THE WRESTLER

**A FILM BY
DARREN ARONOFSKY**

**WRITTEN BY
ROBERT SIEGEL**

**BOOK BY
HI-RES!**

RIZZOLI
NEW YORK

THE WRESTLER

A FILM BY
DARREN ARONOFSKY

WRITTEN BY
ROBERT SIEGEL

BOOK BY
HI-RES!

RIZZOLI
NEW YORK

FADE IN:

MUSIC: QUIET RIOT - "BANG YOUR HEAD (METAL HEALTH)"

Over OPENING CREDITS, a montage of WRESTLING-MAGAZINE
PHOTOS. Action shots of RANDY "THE RAM" ROBINSON from
his '80s WWF heyday. Bodyslamming opponents. Taking
a boot to the face. Headbutting a folding chair held
by a front-row fan. Raising his arms in glorious,
exhausted triumph.

The sounds of a SCREAMING, CHEERING CROWD overwhelm
us. Over the images, various RINGSIDE ANNOUNCERS boom
commentary:

> "...and the Ram is up immediately, throwing
> haymakers and a **piledriver!**"

> "Here tonight on August first, nineteen-eighty-four,
> mark it down! Randy the Ram Robinson..."

> "Eighteen thousand, five hundred fans in the
> nation's capitol! They wanna see the Ram Jam!"

> "March twenty-third, nineteen-eighty-eight, and
> Randy 'The Ram' Robinson set to do battle with
> the Ayatollah."

> "...after slapping The Ram in his face. He doesn't
> realize what this can do to motivate Randy 'The
> Ram' Robinson..."

> "...and it could be time for the Ram Jam. The horns
> are out!
> **The horns are out!**"

The last five or six photos in the montage are from
a match against a keffiyeh-wearing heel named THE
AYATOLLAH before 20,000 screaming fans at Madison
Square Garden...

> "The Beast of the Middle East, the Ayatollah!"

> "The Ayatollah will not let go! He is punishing The
> Ram. My goodness! How much can this man take?!"

> "The Ram stands where we have seen him so many
> times before, playing right to this sold-out
> Madison Square Garden."

> "The horns are out! Here it comes, Ram Jam! My
> goodness! **One, two,** three! **It's over!**"

"...one for the ages, April sixth, nineteen-eighty-nine will forever go down in professional wrestling history!"

A final image of Randy FLYING HIGH ABOVE THE CANVAS, horns out, **poised to crash down on The Ayatollah.**

The Quiet Riot song rings out as we...

DISSOLVE TO:

INT. GARFIELD BOYS AND GIRLS CLUB
- LOCKER ROOM - NIGHT

Present day. Post-match. Randy, pushing 50, still with the same long, dyed-blond mane, sits on a chair in the middle of a classroom. Toys and learning games strewn about around him.

Randy takes a breath. Achy, sweaty, saggy, exhausted. A battered warrior. Scars all over his body. Despite the rough shape he's in, it's clear he's just given it his all in the ring. He takes a swig from a nip of whiskey.

CHYRON: 20 YEARS LATER

He begins to remove his costume. Lime-green ram's horns run up the sides of his wrestling tights. They're the same kind of tights as in the '80s pics - and may well be the actual same pair.

Promoter SCOTT BRUMBERG, a heavyset man in a Mets jersey with BRUMBERG - 44 on the back, approaches.

SCOTT BRUMBERG
Great show, Ram. You really put them over.
Here you go.

He hands Randy some cash. Randy counts it. It's not much.

SCOTT BRUMBERG (CONT'D)
Sorry. I was sure the gate'd be bigger.
But don't forget, two months, Rahway.
Legends signing. I need you, man.

INT. GARFIELD BOYS AND GIRLS CLUB
- SHORT TIME LATER

Randy, changed into his street clothes, limps out of

the school, each step labored and painful. He exits
into the gymnasium where workers take down the ring.
TWO FANS, both men in their 30s, approach him.

                         FAN #1
Yo, Ram. Think you could uh, just sign this for me?

Fan #1 holds out a SHARPIE and a MINI POSTER from the
'80s that features Randy, biceps bulging, crushing a
head of broccoli between his fists. Across the top it
says *EAT YOUR VEGETABLES, PUNK!"*

                         RANDY
                         Sure.

Randy signs the poster, happy to oblige.

                         FAN #2
                    (as Randy signs)
              My first match ever was you versus Davey
                 Diamond at the Spectrum.

                         RANDY
                         Oh, yeah.

                         FAN #1
                    Thanks a lot, man.

Randy hands back the program. FAN #2 hands him
WRESTLING MAGAZINE. On the cover is a shot of Randy
wrestling CORPORAL PUNISHMENT, a heel in a drill in-
structor get-up.

                         #2
              Ninete   y-five.

                         RANDY
              That was a good on

Randy smiles a little. He remembers,   hands
back the poster. Fan #2 looks fondly at Ran   t
of his boyhood.

                         FAN #2
                    (vaguely sad)
              Yeah, you were awesome.

Randy nods, a bit **uncomfortably.**

                         RANDY
              Appreciate it, bro. There you go.

FAN #2
Thanks. Thanks, Ram.

RANDY
(low)
Yeah.

The two fans, muttering thanks, drift back to where
they came from. Randy is left standing alone, still
holding Fan #1's pen.

Randy turns and walks out to the parking lot pulling
his roller bag with him, as a couple of workers take
down the ring.

INT. VAN - SHORT TIME LATER

MUSIC: CINDERELLA - "DON'T KNOW WHAT YOU GOT
(TIL IT'S GONE)"

Randy is driving. On the dashboard is an old ACTION
FIGURE OF HIMSELF from his WWF days. On the stereo
plays a cassette from the 80s.

EXT. MIELEVILLE - RANDY'S TRAILER
- SHORT TIME LATER

Randy parks in front of his TRAILER. He gets out and
heads toward it. He tries to open the front door

                                                             but
it won't budge.

He tugs on the lock. Tugs on the door. No dice. Sees
a large padlock has been put on his trailer.

                    RANDY
                Oh shit.

He walks over and tries the back door. Same problem.

Randy walks over to the MANAGER'S OFFICE across the
way and knocks on the door.

                    RANDY (CONT'D)
                Lenny!

No response. He knocks again.

                    RANDY (CONT'D)
                Lenny!

Still no response. He knocks a little louder.

RANDY (CONT'D)
Come on Lenny. Open up!

He BANGS on the door.

RANDY (CONT'D)
Goddamn it, Lenny!

Frustrated, he gives up and walks back towards his
trailer.

INT. BACK OF VAN - LATER

Randy resignedly climbs into the BACK OF HIS VAN.

The van wall is decorated with a MINI-SHRINE Randy has built to himself. Old magazine and newspa-
per clippings, mini-posters, etc. A few changes of
clothes lie in a messy heap in the corner.

Randy undoes the athletic tape around his elbows. He
grabs a bottle of pills and pops a few, washing them
down with a beer as he contemplates the shrine, long-
ing for his glory days.

CUT TO:

INT. BACK OF VAN - NEXT MORNING

Randy is asleep in his clothes from the night before.
He's STIRRED AWAKE by the sound of kids YELLING and
BANGING on the outside of van.

KID'S VOICE
Ram!

He groans and covers his head with his pillow. Every
inch of him feels like shit.

SECOND KID'S VOICE
Wake up! Ram! Come on!

KID'S VOICE
Ram! Open up!

EXT. MIELEVILLE - SHORT TIME LATER

Randy bursts out of the back of the van.

RANDY
(playfully roars)

Who woke me up!?!

Randy tussles with the group of kids as they call out to be thrown and slammed. He picks one of them up and "chokeslams" him.

                    RANDY (CONT'D)
                    (announcer voice)

Choke slam!

The kids squeal with delight.

As the kids pile on top of him Randy sees a car drive up and park by the MANAGER'S OFFICE. He watches it with interest.

                    RANDY (CONT'D)
          I'll see you maniacs in a little while...

The kids moan with disappointment as Randy heads off towards the manager's trailer.

                    RANDY (CONT'D)
          I'll be back... I'll be back. (to
          himself). I ain't going anyplace.

          EXT. MANAGER'S OFFICE - MOMENTS LATER

Randy runs up to Len, the trailer park's MANAGER, as he opens his front door.

                    RANDY
                    Lenny!

                    LEN THE MANAGER
                    Yeah?

                    RANDY
          Lenny, why are you doing this to me?

                    LEN THE MANAGER
          You'll get in when I get my money.

                    RANDY
          Ah, come on, Lenny. You know I'm always
                    good for it.

                    LEN THE MANAGER
          Yeah. You're good for it every time this
                    happens.

                         RANDY
          Come on, brother. My back went out. Let
          me just at least get my ice packs...

                    LEN THE MANAGER
                  I cannot help you.

                         RANDY
                  Oh, come on, man.

Randy sigh-groans in frustration.

                     RANDY (CONT'D)
                      Oh, God.

        INT. ACME SUPERMARKET- SHORT TIME LATER

Randy walks through the main shopping area into the
stock room, snacking on some red licorice.

                         RANDY
              Hey, Wayne, you got a second?

Up on the ladder is the store manager WAYNE (40) flipping through a loose-leaf binder. He looks down at
Randy, irked.

                         WAYNE
                  Not really. What?

                         RANDY
          Well, I was wondering if you could throw
                 me some more hours.

                         WAYNE
          What's the matter, they raise the price
                     of tights?

Randy chuckles to himself. He secretly hates Wayne.

                         RANDY
                      Funny.

Wayne starts flipping through his binder.

                         WAYNE
              Let's see what we got.

                         RANDY
          Weekdays. I'm busy on the weekends...

CUT TO:

EXT. ACME - REAR LOADING DOCK - DAY

Randy, working alongside some MEXICAN GUYS, lifts a
STACK OF BOXES off the back of a BOAR'S HEAD DELIV-
ERY TRUCK.

He carries the boxes through a RUBBER-STRIP CURTAIN,
into a WALK-IN COOLER. He puts them down and heads
back out again.

CUT TO:

EXT. PIONEER CLUB - LATER

Randy walks up to the Pioneer Club, rolling suitcase
in tow.

INT. PIONEER CLUB - CAFETERIA - SHORT TIME LATER

A makeshift locker room/staging area. 20 or so
WRESTLERS chat as they get into their costumes and
prepare for the upcoming match. Randy and the event's
sleazy, tracksuitclad promoter, NICK VOLPE enter.

                    NICK VOLPE
                    (to Randy)
          You know the boys.

                    WRESTLER #3
          Yo big man! What's up Ram?

                    RANDY
          Hey, what's up?

                    WRESTLER #3
          It's good to see you.

                    RANDY
       Hey bro. Look at you. You're all diesel
          man. (to Burly Blond Wrestler)
          How you doing, brother?

                 BURLY BLOND WRESTLER
          What's going on brother?
          How you been? Good?

                    RANDY
          Good to see you, man.

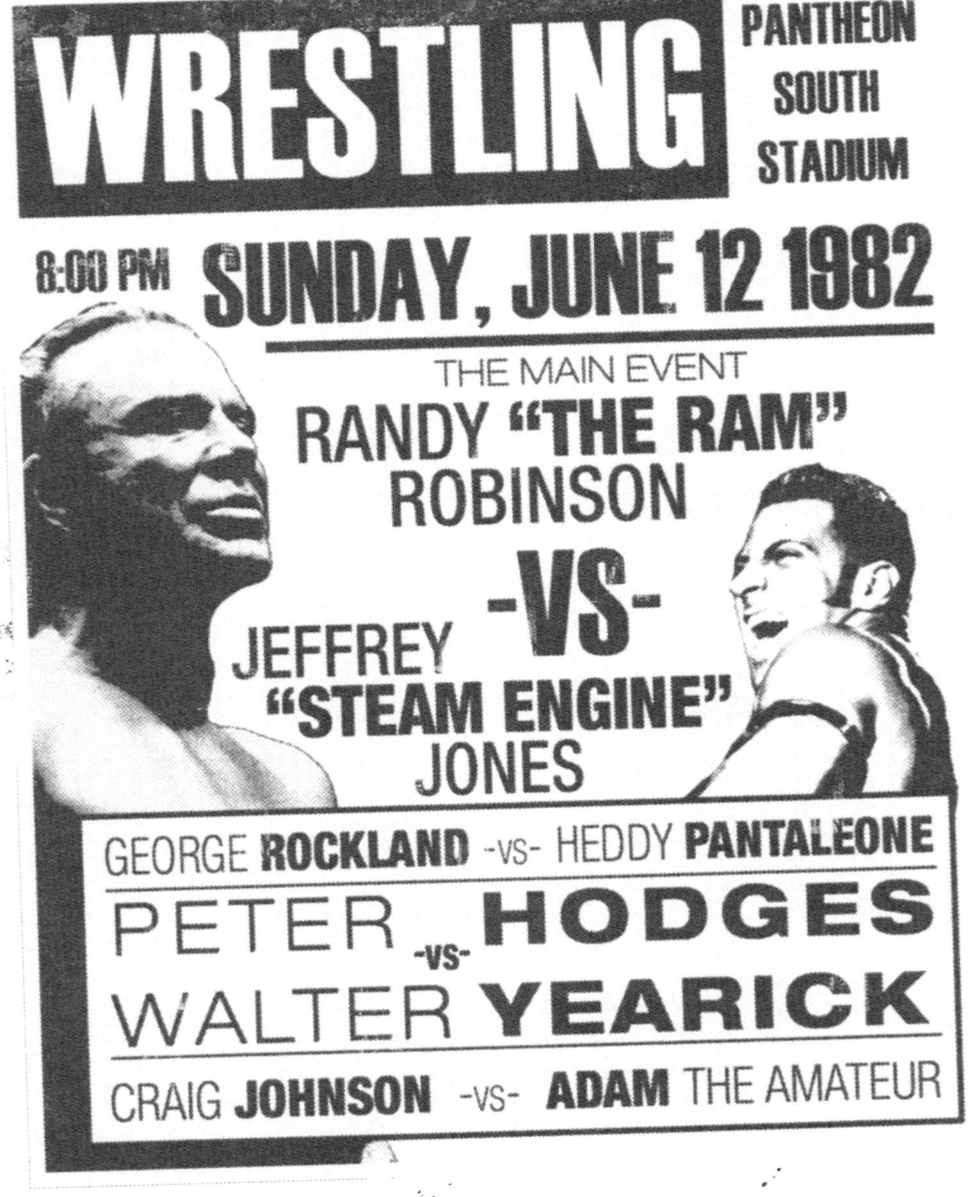
WRESTLING
PANTHEON SOUTH STADIUM
8:00 PM
SUNDAY, JUNE 12 1982
THE MAIN EVENT
RANDY "THE RAM" ROBINSON
-VS-
JEFFREY "STEAM ENGINE" JONES
GEORGE ROCKLAND -VS- HEDDY PANTALEONE
PETER HODGES -VS- WALTER YEARICK
CRAIG JOHNSON -VS- ADAM THE AMATEUR

                          NICK VOLPE
                (ushering Randy into backroom)
             Okay, right here you can change.

Nick returns to address the other wrestlers.

                     NICK VOLPE (CONT'D)
          All right guys, listen up! All right, SLG, where
          are you? You're up first against TDS. Second, we got
                Havoc and Cobian versus Billy the Kid and Lex
                              Lethal. Third...

                          BACKROOM:

Randy starts changing. He takes off his shirt. He's
ripped, still in good shape, if a little stiff in
the joints.

                     NICK VOLPE (O.S.)(CONT'D)
             ...Sabian versus Devan Moore. Fourth,
                  Judas the Traitor versus...

                          CAFETERIA:

                     NICK VOLPE (CONT'D)
          ...Rob Eccos. Intermission. Fifth, Kevin Matthews
          versus Inferno. Sixth, we got Sugar and DJ Hyde
          versus the Funky Samoans. Seventh, Paul E. Nor-
          mous and Andy Anderson versus Jim Powers and Pappa
          Don. And last, but not least, for the strap, we got
          Tommy Rotten versus Randy the Ram. All right, you
                              guys got it?

The wrestlers clap it up in unison, ready for the
match.

                     NICK VOLPE (CONT'D)
             All right, let's do this. Have a good time.

Volpe walks through the double doors to the arena.

     INT. PIONEER CLUB - BACK ROOM - SHORT TIME LATER

Randy is WRAPPING HIS ELBOWS, KNEES AND ANKLES with
athletic tape. He does it in a slow, methodical man-
ner. It feels almost ritualistic.

He is interrupted by a knock on the door from TOMMY
ROTTEN (22) a kid with a punk gimmick who is his
opponent for the evening.

                    TOMMY ROTTEN
                    Hey Ram.

                      RANDY
            Hey there. How you doing man?

                    TOMMY ROTTEN
        Hey. Tommy. I'm gonna be working tonight.

                      RANDY
    I know you Tommy. I saw you out in, uh, Pennsylvania
                a couple months ago.

                    TOMMY ROTTEN
                    Allentown.

                      RANDY
    You were really good, you really brought it.

                    TOMMY ROTTEN
            Thank you. Thank you.

                      RANDY
    Keep working man. You know the people who drive
    the Cadillacs, ones with the politics, they run
    the show. It ain't about ability, so you just hang
                    in there.

                    TOMMY ROTTEN
            Yeah I know, I know.

                      RANDY
                    All right.

                    TOMMY ROTTEN
    But as far as tonight, I don't know what you wanna
    do. I had a few ideas. I was thinking maybe just
    for the heat I would give you a low blow, follow it
                up with a bulldog.

                      RANDY
        Just bring the cheap heat bro.

                  CUT AWAY TO:

                  INT. CAFETERIA

The wrestlers hash out their matches with one another,
discussing their spots, and how they are going to
make things interesting for the crowd.

SAMOAN WRESTLER #1
You guys should get the heat on us right away.

WRESTLER #5A
All right.

SAMOAN WRESTLER #1
Keep the heat on us, beat the shit out of us, **boom,
boom, boom, boom, boom.**

In another part of the room, other wrestlers are
having a similar conversation.

BURLY BLOND WRESTLER
We'll come out, we'll get on the ropes. You guys
bring us both in the hard way.

WRESTLER #6
Okay.

BURLY BLOND WRESTLER
Then we get up, **double drop kick,** we powder out
again. That sounds good.

WRESTLER #6
All right, so we're gonna **really** milk it tonight,
you know?

BURLY BLOND WRESTLER
We're gonna milk it nice and slow, old school,
easy.

WRESTLER #6
Old school.

LEX LETHAL, a massive bald wrestler, lectures the guys.

LEX LETHAL
Don't work his leg, man, that's, everybody does
that. Work his neck. Work his neck.

WRESTLER #7
Yeah, but what's the harm?

WRESTLER #8 (O.S.)
(from another part of the room)
Yo, yo. We're working the neck.

WRESTLER #9 (O.S.)
(from a different part of the room)
We already got the leg.

LEX LETHAL
Oh, you're working the neck? All right. Oh, you
guys got the leg?

WRESTLER #7
You got the leg or the neck, what you got?

CUT BACK TO:

INT. PIONEER CLUB - BACK ROOM

Tommy and Randy continue to discuss their upcoming
match.
TOMMY ROTTEN
Maybe make your comeback right off there.

RANDY
Bang off the ropes, then super kick, then
Ram Jam, and then we go have a beer, okay?

TOMMY ROTTEN
That sounds great man.

RANDY
Okay. You hang in there, you got a lot of ability.

Randy and Tommy exchange thank yous and best wishes.

INT. PIONEER CLUB - BACK ROOM - SHORT TIME LATER

Randy, wearing reading glasses, fidgets with a RAZOR
BLADE. Carefully bending the blade he snaps it in
two. He cuts off a small corner with a pair of
scissors. He places this piece on the top side of his
wrist and wraps it snugly with athletic tape.

Randy pumps himself up, **smashing** his elbows
into his
fists.

INT. PIONEER CLUB - MAIN HALL - SHORT TIME LATER

MUSIC: QUIET RIOT - "BANG YOUR HEAD (METAL HEALTH)"

Randy's intro song plays over the PA system as he
stands behind the curtain waiting for his entrance.
He pumps his fist to the music.

ANNOUNCER
...two hundred twenty-five pounds,

Randy 'The Ram' Robinson!

Randy **busts** through the curtain to the wild cheers **from the crowd.** Randy gives out high fives as he does a lap around the ring. Randy takes a chair from one fan and smashes it over his forehead before sliding into the ring to meet his opponent, Tommy Rotten.

INT. THE RING - CONTINUOUS

Randy and Tommy immediately get to it, **clasping arms,** trying to get one another in a headlock. Randy breaks, grabbing Tommy's arm and flipping him onto the canvas.

Tommy gets back up, only to be thrown back down by Randy. Tommy reverses again, this time, getting Randy in an ARM LOCK, using his bent wrist as leverage to try to force him to the mat. The REFEREE leans in.

> REFEREE
> Hey Ram! Ram? You alright?

> TOMMY ROTTEN
> I'm gonna rip his **arm** off! Check him, ref!

Randy waves him off. The crowd boos at this flagrant ignorance of the rules. The Ref persists.

> REFEREE
> You want me to stop it? You want me to stop it? Are you sure?

Randy puts his hand on the Ref's shoulder, and pushes off, BACK FLIPPING out of the arm lock. Randy pushes Tommy off the ropes and CLOTHESLINES him. Tommy goes down.

Randy struts around the ring, exhorting the crowd, soaking up their cheers. Tommy shoots him a LOW BLOW, Randy doubles over, giving Tommy time to BULLDOG him, grinding Randy's face into the mat. Tommy finishes it with an **ELBOW DROP,** hitting Randy squarely in the chest.

Tommy Rotten lifts Randy up, hoisting him up over his shoulders. Tommy starts to spin him around, slamming Randy's feet into the Ref's head. The Ref goes down, out cold.

Tommy Rotten tightens around Randy's arms, arches his back, presses out his chest and.. WHAM!! He and Randy fly with a LATERAL DROP. Randy's head hits the canvas hard as he slams down on his back.

As Randy writhes on the mat, Tommy Rotten HEADS FOR THE TURNBUCKLE.

RANDY'S POV: Tommy Rotten is untying the turnbuckle's padded cover. Tommy Rotten heads back to Randy. He picks him up by the hair and drags him to the turn buckle, throwing him HEADFIRST into the exposed metal post beneath.

Randy, down on the mat, discretely reaches into his taped up wrist and pulls out the hidden razor blade as Tommy distracts the crowd by throwing the Ref out of the ring.

Randy, clutching his smashed head, discretely runs the blade along his hairline. No one sees it happen.

> TOMMY ROTTEN
> (picks Randy up by the neck)
>
> That's it old man!

Tommy Rotten slams Randy's head into the metal post again. Again. BLOOD STREAMS DOWN Randy's forehead. The crowd's ELECTRIFIED. He tries for another post smash, but HE CAN'T. Randy's neck and arm muscles bulge, he's like Bruce Banner about to become the Hulk. His neck veins pop like he's suddenly supercharged. Tommy tries again, still unable to smash the Ram.

A look of FEAR comes over Tommy Rotten. He knows the tide is about to turn.

Randy throws an elbow, then another. Tommy is done for.

Randy hits Tommy Rotten with everything he's got. Dropkicks. Elbows. Bodyslams. He pours it on, unstoppable.

Randy drags Tommy Rotten into the middle of the ring. He looks out at the crowd. This is what the fans have been waiting for.

> CROWD
> Ram Jam! Ram Jam! Ram Jam!...

The chant quickly spreads.

WHOLE CROWD
RAM JAM! RAM JAM! RAM JAM!...

Randy climbs to the top rope. He plays it up, taunt-
ing the fallen Tommy Rotten.

Randy bends his arms, pressing them against the side
of his head like ram's horns. (Just like in the photo
in the opening montage.)

He **LEAPS.**

The leap is not terribly high or graceful. He **Crashes**
down onto Tommy Rotten horns-first. Tommy Rotten's
whole body **convulses.**

The fans lose it. This is what they wanted. The Ram
Jam. The money shot. The fans chant "ONE...TWO...
THREE!!!!" Along with the ref as Randy pins his op-
ponent.

CUT TO:

INT. CAFETERIA - LATER

Randy, on a post-match high, sits on a ragged couch
as a pseudo-MEDIC stitches up his hairline gash. Nick
Volpe wanders over.

MEDIC
Ram, man, you popped that crowd.
I'm just gonna glue this up, okay?

Randy smiles contentedly. He sure did.

RANDY
Yeah.

NICK VOLPE (O.S.)
Yo, Ram. You got a sec?

RANDY
Come on in.

Nick Volpe comes over.

RANDY (CONT'D)
For you, needledick? Always.

NICK VOLPE
You realize what's coming up?

Randy looks at him, unsure.

                         RANDY
                         Huh?

                    NICK VOLPE
                    April 6th...

Randy racks his brains. He has no idea.

                NICK VOLPE (CONT'D)
20th anniversary of you and Ayatollah at the Garden.

                         RANDY
                        (amazed)
              Hey. Yeah. Long time ago...

                    NICK VOLPE
         Yeah. Time fuckin' flies, right?

Randy sees an excited smile creep across Volpe's
                         face.

                NICK VOLPE (CONT'D)
    Here's what I'm thinking. Two words: Re. Match.

                         MEDIC
                     (finishing up)
         Okay, Ram, you're all set.

Randy is instantly intrigued.

                    NICK VOLPE
Yeah, I'm doing this big Fanfest thing down in Wilmington with Ring of Honor that weekend, I wanna main
event it with you two guys. "Ram, Ayatollah Two".

                         RANDY
Hey, I heard Bob was doing really good with his
used car lot out in Arizona. I don't know if he's
              gonna want, you know...

                    NICK VOLPE
For this, Bob's gonna dust off the old turban.

                         RANDY
                         Yeah?

                    NICK VOLPE
                    Yeah.

                         RANDY
                      Hey, bring it.

INT. CAFETERIA - SHORT TIME LATER

Randy exits the backroom to WHOOPS and HOLLERS from
his fellow wrestlers, in awe of this old-timer that
just gave his all in the ring.

                     WRESTLER #10A
                     That's for Ram!

                     WRESTLER #10B
                         Ram!

                     WRESTLER #10C
                 Good stuff. Good stuff man.

                     WRESTLER #11
                  Just like the old days.

                         RANDY
                        (joking)
      Come on guys, let's all go take a shower together.

                        CUT TO:

EXT. CHEEQUES- PARKING LOT - SHORT TIME LATER

A spring in his hobbled step, Randy gets out of the
van and heads toward Cheeques, the strip club he
passed earlier. Manning the door is BIG CHRIS, a huge
bouncer/doorman.

                       BIG CHRIS
               What's up, Ram? How you doing?

                         RANDY
               What's up, Big Chris, what's shaking?

                       BIG CHRIS
      I'm all right. They chummily shake hands. Big Chris
                pulls Randy in tight.

                   BIG CHRIS (CONT'D)
                    (into Randy's ear)
             Yo, baby, you still got that hook up with
              the quack at your gym? The juice head?

                         RANDY
                  What do you need?

                    BIG CHRIS
        Yo, my back is still killing. Vicodine, percs,
             Nubain, whatever he's got.

                    RANDY
    Come by the mansion in a couple of days, I'll hook
                    it up.

                    BIG CHRIS
        Ah, you the man, Ram. You the man.

Randy enters the club.

            INT. CHEEQUES- SHORT TIME LATER

        MUSIC: BIRDMAN & LIL WAYNE - "STUNTIN' LIKE MY
                    DADDY"

    A crowded, not-very-glamorous Jersey strip club.
    Randy heads over to the bar.

                    RANDY
            Hey, Ruby. How you doing, baby?

                    RUBY
            Hey, Ram. How's it going?

                    RANDY
                    (sighs)
            I'll take a cold one.

                    RUBY
                All right.

    The female BARTENDER slides him a beer.

                    RUBY(CONT'D)
            There you go.

    Randy takes a swig, looking around the club.

                    RANDY
            Cassidy around?

                    BARTENDER
            I think she's VIP-in'

                    RUBY
        I think she's working the VIP.

    INT. CHEEQUES- MEN'S ROOM - MOMENTS LATER

MUSIC: SAMSAYA - "Dodge It"

Randy is at the urinal. He flushes and heads over to
the sink. He washes his hands, checking his look in
the mirror. He primps a little.

INT. CHEEQUES- MAIN ROOM - CONTINUOUS

Randy exits the bathroom and heads back toward the
bar. En route, he passes a curtained-off VIP ROOM.

                    WOMAN (O.S.)
        Trust me, babe. You're gonna be so happy.

Randy, hearing this, slows.

                    DUDE #1 (O.S.)
        I'm sorry, sweetie. We said the other girl.

                    DUDE #2 (O.S.)
        Yeah, the blonde girl with the belly chain. Yeah,
                    the other girl.

Randy peeks through the curtain. Inside, he sees
CASSIDY(36), a sexy, tattooed, aging rocker chick in
a white spandex dress. With her are six hair-gelled,
goombahwannabe BACHELOR-PARTY DUDES (early 20s). The
BACHELOR is sitting in a chair in the middle.

                    CASSIDY
        The other girl. Oh? Well, yeah, but she's on break.

                    DUDE #1
                    (laughing)
        Yeah, yeah. Look, well, I'm sorry, but we really
                    don't want you.

                    DUDE #3
                How old are you, anyway?

                    DUDE #1
            Oh. You're like my mom's age.

Stifled laughter from his buddies.

ON the other side of curtain:

Randy's anger builds as he watches.

Vip room: Cassidy, trying to salvage the gig, strad-
dles the bachelor.

                    CASSIDY
          Hey, there's nothing like experience.
              (into his ear, seductive)
    I do things your fiancee's never even dreamed of doing.

                  DUDE #3 (O.S.)
                   Yeah, right.

                    DUDE #4
                   Oh, what!

                    DUDE #2
          Yeah, like graduate in 1985.

This cracks his friends up. Randy BURSTS THROUGH THE
CURTAIN.

                    RANDY
    Hey, hey, hey. You girls are being a little rude to
        the lady. How about an apology, huh?

Everyone is taken aback, including Cassidy.

                    DUDE #2

     Who the fuck are you, man?

                   CASSIDY
                     Oh!

                    RANDY

 Don't talk to the lady like that.

                   CASSIDY
             Oh, wait a second.

                    DUDE #2

  I'll talk to her like I wanna talk to her.

Cassidy wedges herself between Randy and Dude #2.

                   CASSIDY
    No, it's okay. Thanks, thanks, thanks.

                    RANDY
**You don't need to be talking to her like that. No,
  it's not okay, baby, it's definitely not okay.**

                   CASSIDY
     It's cool. It's cool. I got it. I got it. I got
    it. It's all right, guys. It's all right. It's all
                    right.

YouYou

He turns to the bachelor.

Randy gives her a cheesy smile...

(laughing)
I didn't mean it...

CUT:TO:

RANDY (CONT'D)

thing. Knowing better,

RANDY (low, out)

          Hey, I was just trying to help. Oh, come on.
          They were punks!

you the man, Ram,

RANDY

He turns to the bachelor.

the club.

of you.

CHEEQUE SH

feel

LIL WAYNE

DADDY

down next   him. A ne

glamorou   ers   rip

PITBULL   "UNA MANO I A LA OTRA"

NDY

CUT: TO
RANDY (CONT'D)

ing. Knowing better,

RAND   'D) t   ing?

knows? (o   in pretty

know, wi   a little luc   ould

be my ticke back on to

supportively sincere!

CAS IDY

know wh 's ir   owd.

he female

RANDY

ah. Th t   d be a dream.

Hey, I was just trying to help. Oh, come on.
They were punks!

arts   ver speaker):   the club.

Randy   s a sw   R   "N2 Sumthin' "

He turns to the bachelor.

                    RANDY
No, no, let me tell you **something**. I guarantee you,
this lady's a **hundred times hotter** than **any** skank-
ass pussy you're gonna be marrying.

                    CASSIDY
                   (sighing)
                     Oh.

                    DUDE #2
                  (to Dudes)
What the fuck? That's my fucking sister.

                    DUDE #3
                   What?!

                    RANDY
            What'd you say?

Dude #1 steps to Randy, **chest puffed out**.

                RANDY (CONT'D)
                 Bitch!

RANDY pushes into the dudes challenging them to start
something. Knowing better, the DUDES leave, dragging
angry DUDE #1 with them.

                    DUDE #1
               (on the way out)
Are you fucking kiddin' me? Are you kidding me?

                    RANDY
             (on DUDES exit)
          Motherfucker!
                   CASSIDY
               See you soon.

Randy looks at Cassidy, expecting a hearty thank you.
Instead he gets a PISSED-OFF SHOVE.

                CASSIDY (CONT'D)
     Two hundred fucking bucks walked out.

Randy is totally taken aback.

                    RANDY
    Hey, I was just trying to help. Oh, come on.
              They were punks!

34

CASSIDY picks up a chair and CASSIDY half-jokingly
swings the chair at RANDY.

                    RANDY(CONT'D)
               Hey, whoa. Easy there.

                    CASSIDY
               You!

Randy gives her a cheesy smile.

                    RANDY
          I'm sorry. I'm better-looking than them anyway.

CASSIDY laughs.
                    RANDY (CONT'D)
                    (laughing)
          I didn't mean to piss you off. Come on.

                    CASSIDY
          Yeah, okay. (chuckles) It's good to see you man.

                    RANDY
               Good to see you. Goddamn.

                    CASSIDY
          I haven't seen you in a while. How you been?

She gives him a warm smile.

                    CUT TO:

          INT. CHEEQUES- SHORT TIME LATER

          MUSIC: KHIA - "MY NECK, MY BACK"

Randy is getting a LAPDANCE from CASSIDY, she stands
between his open legs.

                    RANDY
          Now, I'm telling you, it was one of the historic
          matches in history. (off) It was twenty thousand
          people. Another million and a half sitting at home
          watching on pay-per-view. We're slamming the piss
          out of each other. I mean, for God knows how long
          we're both gassing. You ask any old wrestling fan,
               they've heard about that one.

She climbs on top of him, her naked body just inches
from his face.

CASSIDY
Million and a half? Shit.

RANDY
Yeah, it was big. And a rematch...
(smiles, contemplating the prospect)
Hey, this could be history all over again.

Cassidy leans back giving Randy a full view of her body.

RANDY (CONT'D)
Goddamn, look at you. You are one smoking baby. Let me make an honest woman out of you.

Cassidy smiles a little. This makes her feel good.

"My Neck My Back" ENDS. Cassidy pulls back on her dress and casually sits down next to him. A new song comes on.

MUSIC: PITBULL - "UNA MANO LAVA LA OTRA"

They look toward the stage, where a PUERTO RICAN STRIPPER shakes her ass to the staccato, abrasive Latin rap song.

RANDY (CONT'D)
I mean, who knows? I'm in pretty good shape right now. You know, with a little luck, this could be my ticket back on top.

Cassidy nods supportively, sincerely.

CASSIDY
You never know who's in that crowd.

RANDY
Yeah. (low) Yeah. That would be a dream.

MUSIC (starts over speaker):
TAKBIR BASHIR - " N2 Sumthin' "

An ALARMED LOOK comes over Cassidy's face.

CASSIDY
Oh, Jesus, you're bleeding. (sighing) Oh.
Randy follows her eyes to his HAIRLINE. A small amount of BLOOD is trickling down from his stitches. He grabs a COCKTAIL NAPKIN and casually dabs it.

                    RANDY
          Yeah, I got cut tonight.

                    CASSIDY
               You okay?

                    RANDY
          Yeah, it's nothing.

                    CASSIDY
               (small chuckle)
          They say wrestling's fake, huh?

Randy proudly holds out his arm.

                    RANDY
          Fake? I'll show you fake.

Randy rolls up his sleeve to reveal a nasty SCAR on
his bicep.

                    RANDY (CONT'D)
Look at this, nineteen-eighty-six, Denver Coliseum.
Billy Bob Banjo hit me with a two-by-four. It had
a loose nail in it, split my bicep right the hell
               open. Look at that.

Cassidy admires it.

                    RANDY (CONT'D)
          I got a better one than that.

He pulls down his shirt collar, revealing an even
nastier COLLARBONE SCAR.

                    RANDY (CONT'D)
Take a look at this here. Nineteen-eighty-eight, at
the Orlando Civic Center. Mr. Magnificent threw me
over the top ropes. I landed on my shoulder and
          cracked my clavicle right in half.

                    CASSIDY
               Oh my god.

                    RANDY
               Yeah.

                    CASSIDY
          Doesn't it hurt?

                    RANDY

                      39

Well, it hurts when I breathe, but, I mean, you
know, you hear the roar of the crowd, you just, you
just, you pull through, you know?

Cassidy gazes soulfully at the scar.

> CASSIDY
> "He was pierced for our transgressions, He was
> crushed for our iniquities. The punishment that
> brought us peace was upon Him, and by His wounds we
> were healed."

Randy contemplates the quote.

> RANDY
> What was that all about?

> CASSIDY
> It's from "Passion of the Christ". *(touching his
> hair)* You have the same hair. You never seen it?

Randy shrugs no.

> CASSIDY (CONT'D)
> Dude, you gotta! It's, it's amazing. They throw
> everything at him: whips, arrows, rocks. They beat
> the living fuck out of him the whole two hours. He
> just takes it.

> RANDY
> Tough dude.

Cassidy lightly traces a finger along Randy's clavcle
scar.

> CASSIDY
> Sacrificial Ram!

She cracks herself up.

> CLUB D.J. (O.S.)
> Next on the main stage will be Cassidy, with
> Harmony on the small stage.

> CASSIDY
> *(low to him)*
> Oh. Ah, fuck. Gotta go.

> RANDY
> Where you going?

Cassidy stands up. She begins gathering her things

and slips on a see-through shirt.

                    RANDY (CONT'D)
                  What do I owe you?

He reaches into his pocket and finds a wad of cash.

                    CASSIDY
                  That's sixty.

Randy peels off three $20s and hands them to her.

                    RANDY
                  Keep the change.

                    CASSIDY
                  Thank you.

She leaves.
                    RANDY
              (touching his forehead wound)
                  Goddamn.

INT. CHEEQUES - STAGE - SHORT TIME LATER

MUSIC: FIREHOUSE - " Don't Walk Away "

                    CLUB D.J. (O.S.)
              ...to the stage the lovely Cassidy!

Cassidy BURSTS ONTO THE STAGE. She owns it with rock
'n' roll energy.

                    CUT TO:

INT. DOLPHIN FITNESS CENTER- LOCKER ROOM - DAY

Randy sits with GREGG, a huge bodybuilder who has
laid out an assortment of steroids and pharmaceuti-
cals. Another LARGE BODY BUILDER stands at the door
keeping watch.

                    GREGG
    Bottle of Anadrol, two-fifty, bottle of EQ, sev-
   enty-five bucks, two bottles of Trend, seventy-five
     dollars each, buckfifty, bottle of Insulin, hun-
   dred bucks. You got four boxes of Sustanon. There's
      three amps in a box, thirty dollars on a box, a
   buck-twenty. A bottle of D-Ball, hundred bucks. For
    your bitch tits I got you a bottle of Rimidex, two
      hundred bucks. All together, nine ninety-five.

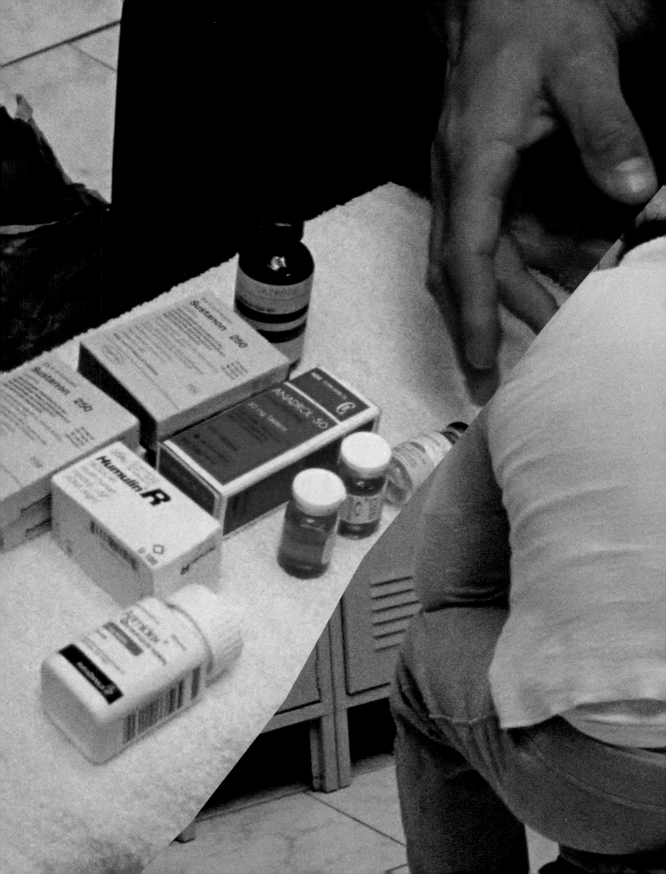

GREGG (CONT'D)
I know you only got four hundred. Give me the four
hundred. I know you're good for the rest.

RANDY
You got any GH?

GREGG
Got Chinese and I got Zorastin.

RANDY
I don't want any of that Chinese stuff.

GREGG
My boy, Ram. I'll hook you up, all right?

RANDY
(chuckling)
Okay.

Gregg begins stuffing a sack with all the drugs Randy
has bought.

GREGG
You gotta take the bacteriostatic water with it,
too. It makes the growth last longer. Need anything
else? Painkillers? Vics? Percs?

RANDY
No, bro, I'm tapped.

GREGG
Demerol? Oxycontins? Sure?

RANDY
No, this'll do me.

GREGG
Viagra?

RANDY
No.

GREGG
Maybe some blow?
Got it all man. Whatever you need, you know.

RANDY
You should open up a pharmacy brother.

GREGG

You're my man, I gotta look out for you, you know.

                    RANDY
              I'm square.

                    GREGG
Just need the juice and you're all right man right?

                    RANDY
    Yeah. I'm just gonna get big and strong. Yeah.

                    GREGG
         Yes you are my friend.

                    RANDY
      Okay. We're done, okay.

                    GREGG
      All right. Anytime, man.

Randy admires Gregg's physique.

                    RANDY
      You looking good brother.

                    GREGG
    I'm trying, baby, I'm trying.

                    RANDY
    Show me what you got there.

                    GREGG
    Ah, come on man, come on.

                    RANDY
Come on, show me, come on, bro, show me what you got.

Gregg flexes, showing off his enormous arm and chest
muscles.

                    GREGG
      Just a little something.
    There's not much there, baby.

                    RANDY
    Up, up. Bring it up. Bring it up.
    Bring it up. Look at that, motherfucker.

GREGG laughs.

INT. LOCKER ROOM - TOILET STALL - SHORT TIME LATER

                        45

Randy, underwear pulled down, plunges a needle into
his ass cheek.

INT. GYM FLOOR - SHORT TIME LATER

MUSIC: RHINOBUCKET - "Soundtrack to a War"

Randy alone, lifting free weights, working his arms.
He grunts loudly as he squeezes out one more rep.

INT. COLOR AND CUTS - SHORT TIME LATER

MUSIC: VALERIE BISHARAT - "Nice Guys Finish First"

Randy sits in a chair as a Korean HAIR DRESSER wearing latex gloves BLEACHES HIS ROOTS. His hair is full
of plastic clips.

> RANDY
> Okay, right up there. See, right up there, what
> you're doing right there? Don't leave the foils on
> too long, because last time they broke off. I think
> they got too fried.

The Hair Dresser responds in Korean.

> RANDY (CONT'D)
> Yeah. I got it.
> So how's the old man doing these days?

She answers him.

> RANDY (CONT'D)
> Yeah?

> HAIR DRESSER
> Work, work, work.

> RANDY
> Work, work, work. Well, hey, hm, at least he's got
> a job, right?

INT. TROPICAL TANNING - LATER

A strip-mall tanning salon. Randy breezes in, nodding
hello to the FRONT-DESK WOMAN, who's on the phone.

> RANDY
> Hey, Gloria. How you doing?

> FRONT-DESK WOMAN

(cupping phone)
Hey, babe. Five's open.

INT. TROPICAL TANNING - SHORT TIME LATER

ANGLE ON a tanning pod. With some trouble RANDY
strips down to his underwear, puts on protective
goggles and gets in the pod.

CUT TO:

EXT. JERSEY DOLLAR - SHORT TIME LATER

RANDY and LEX LETHAL park in front of a strip-mall
99- Cent store.

LEX LETHAL
Thanks again for the lift bro.

RANDY
You got it.

INT. JERSEY DOLLAR - SHORT TIME LATER

A Long Island strip-mall 99-CENT STORE. Randy and Lex
browse an aisle. Randy picks up a TIN COOKIE SHEET.

LEX LETHAL
(pointing to his forehead)
Here you go. Lay it on brother. Lay it on.

Randy bangs it against his forehead, testing it out.
It makes a LOUD CLANG.

LEX LETHAL (CONT'D)
There you go.

RANDY
(laughing)
Ah. You're supposed to fall to your knees.
(sighs)
All right, good.

Lex laughs.

RANDY (CONT'D)
(to the cashier)
Hey, where's the bug spray in here?

CASHIER
Lane six to the right side.

                         RANDY
                         Huh?

                         CASHIER
                    The right side, bottom.

                         RANDY
                 Right side, bug spray?

                    SHORT TIME LATER

Lex and Randy are looking at pots and pans. Randy
picks up a small frying pan.

                    RANDY (CONT'D)
                   (motioning to pan)
                         Hm?

Whacks Lex in the back.

                       LEX LETHAL
                 Go ahead, once more.

Randy whacks him again harder. Then gives the pan to
Lex.

                         RANDY
                Now give it to me brother.

                       LEX LETHAL
                    All right man.

Lex slams the pan down on Randy's back, accidentally
breaking off the handle. The pan CLATTERS to the
floor.

                         RANDY
                 Fuck. Come on, let's go.

                    SHORT TIME LATER

Different aisle, different weapons.

                    RANDY (CONT'D)
                  Couple mouse traps?

                       LEX LETHAL
         Load them and set them in the ring, body slam.

                         RANDY
                     Let's do it.

They throw a bunch of mousetraps in their shopping
basket.

At the check-out the CASHIER looks up at the big
hulks as he rings them up.

                    RANDY (CONT'D)
              How you doing sir?

                    CASHIER
              How you doing?

                    LEX LETHAL
              What's going on my man?

                    RANDY
              Tell me, what do you think?
              What do you think about this? Huh?

Randy takes a couple of plastic pot covers and
pretends to box Lex's ears with them. Lex reacts,
convulsing with mock pain.

                    LEX LETHAL
              That'll work.

                    RANDY
              Okay.
                    (to cashier)
              Come here.

He playfully swats at the Cashier as he did with Lex.
The Cashier plays along, to Randy and Lex's amusement.

                    CUT TO:

INT. NEW ALHAMBRA ARENA - GYM - LATER

Randy watching from BEHIND A CURTAIN as a ROWDY CROWD
of about 300 fills a COMMUNITY-CENTER GYM. The vibe of
the crowd is a bit rougher than previous events.

In the ring four BLOODY WRESTLERS attack each other
ruthlessly.

INT. DRESSING AREA

RANDY and his opponent NECRO BUTCHER hash out their
upcoming match.

                    NECRO BUTCHER

I don't look good, but I feel good.

                    RANDY
               Yeah?

                    NECRO BUTCHER
     So, my-my knees, my back, anything you need me to
     do, sir, just maybe, uh, keep the running to a min-
     imum, like maybe I could hit the ropes once, take a
     bump for you, but, like, no criss-crossing, please.

                    RANDY
     Uh-huh. Yeah. Hardcore stuff, I mean, what do you,
     talk to me about it. What do you wanna do tonight?

                    NECRO BUTCHER
        Well, oh, are you cool with the staples?

                    RANDY
                 Uh, staples?

                    NECRO BUTCHER
                 Staple gun.

                    RANDY
              What do you mean?

                    NECRO BUTCHER
            (motioning as if he were
            stapling Randy's chest)
            Like... staple gun.

                    RANDY
               Staple gun.

                    NECRO BUTCHER
        You, you never did it before?

                    RANDY
        Oh, no... Does that hurt? Huh.

                    NECRO BUTCHER
     Sort of a silly question, but, yeah. Man, uh, not
              so bad going in.

                    RANDY
               Yeah.

                    NECRO BUTCHER
        Kind of scary. You know, you got a big
        metal thing up against you, but...

                    52

                         RANDY
                     Yeah... well...

                      NECRO BUTCHER
Pulling them out, they're gonna leave a couple little holes, a little bit of blood loss there, but...

                         RANDY
                      (accepting)
              Yeah. Yeah. Rock and roll.

They shake hands.

                      NECRO BUTCHER
          Thank you, sir. It's an honor. Thank you.

                         RANDY
          Take it easy with that staple gun.

                      NECRO BUTCHER
                      (chuckles)
                   No problem sir.

                        CUT TO:

              INT. THE RING - 1 HOUR LATER

RANDY and NECRO BUTCHER in the ring. Necro untangles
himself from a broken table covered in barb wire
and gets up only to be smashed over the head with a
plate glass window. It explodes and Necro falls to
the mat.

A bloody Randy wearily pins Necro. ONE TWO THREE!

Victorious Randy shoots his arms up. The crowd goes
crazy.

                      RING ANNOUNCER #1
                      (over loudspeaker)
              Ladies and gentlemen, your winner, the
              legend, Randy "The Ram" Robinson!

After he collects his cheers, the Ram, still out of
breath, stumbles out of the ring and back towards the
DRESSING AREA.

A haggard and bloodied RANDY enters to the cheers of
his fellow wrestlers.

                        MEDIC
              Great show Ram. Good job.

                    AWED WRESTLER #1
                      There he is.

A MEDIC sits him down and starts to clean him up.
Various wrestlers congratulate him. Necro Butcher is
nearby cleaning himself up.

The Ram bums a cigarette and a beer.

                 AWED WRESTLER #1 (CONT'D)
          Hell of a match out there, man. Hell of
          a match. Put yourself through hell, man.
                    That was great.

                        RANDY
                      Thank you.

                    AWED WRESTLER #2
              Great. Good work. Way to go.

Randy coughs.

                    AWED WRESTLER #3
              It was fucking insane Ram.

                        MEDIC
        (attending to a large deep gash on Randy's side)
              Let me just get some glue for that.

                    AWED WRESTLER #4
              Crazy shit man. Crazy.

                        RANDY
                  (to Necro Butcher)
          Hey. You okay with that table hit?

                    NECRO BUTCHER
              I'll live sir... I'll live.

                        RANDY
                        Yeah.

Randy smirks, pondering his performance.

                      CUT TO:

THE START OF THE MATCH - FOURTEEN MINUTES EARLIER

Randy and Necro Butcher sit on folding chairs in the center of the ring facing each other. Under Necro Butcher's chair is his canvas sack. Under Randy's is his Dollar Tree plastic shopping bag.

Necro Butcher slaps Randy across the face. Randy slaps Necro Butcher. They take turns hitting each other, each shot a little harder than the last. It's like a violent game of "slaps."

After a stretch of this, Necro Butcher reaches into his sack and pulls out a can of BUG SPRAY. He SPRAYS it in Randy's face.

CUT BACK TO:

LATER AFTER THE MATCH - BACKSTAGE

As the medics continue to clean Randy and the Necro Butcher up, One medic pries staples out of the Ram's chest.

RANDY
Ah, shit!

MEDIC #2
You got a lot of staples, we gotta take them out

RANDY
Fuck Take it easy doc.

MEDIC #2
Hold still.

The medic takes another one out.

RANDY
Ow! Goddamn it, fuck...

A different Medic pries a stapled 5 DOLLAR BILL off of Necro's forehead.

GO BACK TO:

MINUTES AGO IN THE RING

Necro Butcher grabs a staplegun from his sack. He staples a five dollar bill to his forehead, and then staples his chest and arms.

Then he turns on Randy and staples him on the chest
and on the head.

Necro reaches down into a tray of silverware and
pulls out a FORK, holding it up for the crowd.

> NECRO BUTCHER
> It's dinner time.

He grabs Randy's hair and sticks it in The Ram's
forehead drawing blood. Randy cries out in pain.

> RANDY
> Goddamn it.

Randy forces Necro's hand away, reaches and grabs an
aluminum COOKIE TRAY. He swings around and smacks
Necro Butcher in the face with it, knocking him back
out of the ring. The tray makes an awesomely loud
METALLIC CLANG.

> OUTSIDE THE RING:

Randy WHALES NECRO BUTCHER IN THE FACE with a barb-
wire covered crutch. Necro Butcher stumbles back-
wards toward the metal barricade between the ring and
the fans. Randy kicks him in the chest. Necro Butcher
flips over the barricade, into the crowd. Fans scatter
in an exhilarated panic.

Randy follows after him. He throws Necro Butcher into
a row of empty chairs. Necro Butcher goes sprawling.
Chairs fly everywhere.

Randy's heart is beating LOUD. FAST.

Dazed, he heads toward the SNACK-BAR AREA. NECRO
BUTCHER follows after him. Randy grabs a metal GARBAGE
CAN and WHIPS AROUND WITH IT, smacking Necro Butcher
square in the face. Necro Butcher goes down.

Randy shakes out the can's contents over Necro Butcher,
showering him in trash. He shoves Necro Butcher's head
into the can. Randy picks up a folding chair, holds it
up to the crowd for approval. The crowd goes wild.

Then an AMPUTEE offers his prosthetic leg to Randy.

> MAN #4 IN CROWD
> Ram, use his leg! Use his leg!

MAN WITH PROSTHETIC LEG
Use it! Use my leg! Yeah!

CROWD
(chanting)
Use his leg! Use his leg!

Randy takes the leg to even more wild cheers, winds
up and broadsides Necro. He hits the floor.

MAN #5 IN CROWD
Fuck you, Necro, fuck you!

Randy clambers over the barrier back towards the
ring. Necro gets up and surprises him with a blow to
the back with a folding chair.

RETURN TO:

AFTER THE MATCH - BACKSTAGE

Ram holds a grungy washcloth to his forehead, trying
to ease his headache. The medic plucks out the two
dozen metal tacks and pieces of glass that stick in
the Ram's back.

RETURN TO:

INT. THE RING - 10 MINUTES AGO

Randy is thrown through a large piece of plate
glass wrapped in barb wire. It explodes, glass flies
everywhere. He falls to his knees and tenderly picks
a strand of barb wire out of a LARGE GASH in his
side.

RETURN TO:

AFTER THE MATCH - BACKSTAGE

The medic super glues shut the large gash. Randy
hacks and splutters, throws up in his mouth a little
from the pain.

RETURN TO:

THE RING - 15 MINUTES AGO

Necro slams Randy repeatedly with a water cooler
bottle attached to the end of a long pole.

Stunned, Randy lies in a pile of glass and blood while Necro sets up a twelve foot ladder in the center of the ring. It is surrounded by tables covered with barbed wire and tacks.

Necro Butcher drags Randy by his hair up the ladder rung by rung.

At the top of the ladder he prepares to push Randy off.

But Randy counters. He surprises him with a punch to the stomach. Necro Butcher is caught totally off guard.

Randy grabs Necro Butcher and PUSHES OFF causing Necro Butcher to CRASH THROUGH THE TABLE with Randy on top of him. Randy savagely beats the fallen Necro Butcher.

                    RETURN TO:

        AFTER THE FIGHT - BACKSTAGE - RIGHT NOW

The MEDIC finishes up his work on Randy, who is quiet, head in hands.

                    MEDIC #2
                   (leaving)
    Okay, Ram, you're good. Go take a shower.

Randy stands up, walks a few steps toward the shower room. He hesitates, then vomits. He massages his left arm. Something is wrong. He looks around concerned. No one is looking at him.

His knees buckle and he collapses on the ground.

               MEDIC #2 (CONT'D)
                 Ram! Ram!

                FADE TO BLACK.

        INT. POST-OP RECOVERY ROOM - NEXT DAY

Randy lies asleep in a hospital bed, an oxygen tube in his nose.

His eyes slowly open. He looks around, disoriented. Woozy. Confused by all the wires on him, he starts PULLING THINGS OFF. Monitors BEEP. Nurses rush into

the room, calming him down as they try to reattach
the wires.

                    NURSE #1
        Just try and relax. Just try and relax.
                  (to NURSE #2)
        Marlene, can I have some help in here please?

Randy feebly fi g h t s her away.

                    NURSE #1 (CONT'D)
        Put your arms down. Okay, try and relax.

Randy continues to fight. A second nurse arrives and
injects a sedative into Randy's IV.

                    NURSE #1 (CONT'D)
        Okay, very good. Calm down.

Randy slowly passes out and the nurses reattach his
wires.

                    NURSE #1(CONT'D)
        Okay. Thanks Marlene.

        INT. ROBERT WOOD HOSPITAL -
        POST-OP RECOVERY ROOM - NIGHT

Randy lies unconscious. There's a BREATHING TUBE in
his mouth and ANOTHER TUBE going through his CHEST
WALL. He's hooked up to a MECHANICAL VENTILATOR.

        INT. RANDY'S ROOM - NEXT DAY

Randy, transferred to a regular hospital room, is
trying to stand up.

                    MAN'S VOICE (O.S.)
                 (slight Indian accent)
                  Mr. Ramzinski.

Randy looks up. DR. MOAYEDIZADEH (40) enters the room.

                    RANDY
                Call me Randy.

                    DR. MOAYEDIZADEH
        Randy, I'm Dr. Moayedizadeh.

                    RANDY
        So how we lookin', doc?

                    DR. MOAYEDIZADEH
          Well, much better than before the bypass.

                         RANDY
                        (sighs)
          So we're in the clear, we're all good?

From the doctor's face, it's not quite that simple.

                    DR. MOAYEDIZADEH
          Well it's your heart, you need to start taking bet-
                    ter care of it.

                         RANDY
               Like how? What do I do?

                    DR. MOAYEDIZADEH
          Well, for starters, you're going to be on
          a slew of medications. And the stuff your putting
              in your body, you need to cut it out.

                         RANDY
          I know. I know. I can do without that. When can I
              get back in the gym and start working out?

                    DR. MOAYEDIZADEH
          As far as exercise goes, it's still okay as long as
                    it's moderate.

A beat.

                         RANDY
                        (firm)
               Doc, I'm a professional wrestler.

                    DR. MOAYEDIZADEH
               That's not a good idea.

                         RANDY
                  What do you mean?

                    DR. MOAYEDIZADEH
          Your heart's been through a lot, it won't handle
                    strenuous activity.

                         RANDY
          Well I can slow my routine down, I can pace myself...

                    DR. TARACHANDANI
               Mr. Ramzinski...

RANDY

...we're ...

...ce, ...s not q...

MOAYEDIZADEH
you need
...care of...

RANDY
...ke how? Wha...

DR. MOA...
...or starters...
...of medications...
...in your body,...

I know. I know. I...
get back in...

far as exer... bea...

Doc, I'm a...

DR. MO...
...That's not...

RANDY
...What do you me...

...MOAYEDIZADEH
...ugh a lot, it
...activity.

...n pace my
...ough a lot, I won't

ndy, .

v, doc. Thank:

NT. RANDY'S ROO.

ns, wearing h
of tights

AL -

ork.

The ADMISSI
He folds it up a

RD,

ADMISSION

out $50

TIME LATF

o the brigh
adjusting. H
animal.

RA ARENA - PARKING
HORT TIME LATER

                    RANDY
                  (pleading)
            Randy. Call me Randy.

               DR. TARACHANDANI
     Randy, you almost died. Next time you might not be
                     so lucky.

                    RANDY
                  (sarcastic)
       Well, hey, doc. Thanks for all the good news.

             INT. RANDY'S ROOM - LATER

Randy packs up his things, wearing his street clothes.
He finds his ripped-up pair of tights and throws them
away.

             INT. ROBERT WOOD HOSPITAL -
             ADMISSIONS DESK - MORNING

Randy is checking out of the hospital.

               ADMISSIONS-DESK WOMAN
                This copy's for you.

The ADMISSIONS-DESK WOMAN hands him some paperwork.
He folds it up and stuffs it in a pocket.

               ADMISSIONS-DESK WOMAN
                     (CONT'D)
           And somebody left this for you.
             He said he was your promoter.

She hands him a plain white ENVELOPE. Randy opens it.
Inside is a NOTE:

YOU EARNED IT DUDE... YOUR A WARRIOR! REST UP, FEEL
BETTER. ——JERRY DIFUSCO PS... IF YOUR UP BY THE 23RD,
I GOT SOMETHING IN YONKERS

Randy looks into the envelope again and pulls out $500.

          EXT. ROBERT WOOD HOSPITAL - SHORT TIME LATER

Randy steps out of the hospital into the bright light
of day. He squints, his eyes adjusting. He stands
there looking around, a lost animal.

          EXT. NEW ALHAMBRA ARENA - PARKING LOT -
                  SHORT TIME LATER

A CAB pulls up to Randy's van, still parked in the
community center's lot. Randy steps out of the cab
and limps to the van.

INT. DRUG FAIR PHARMACY - SHORT TIME LATER

Randy roams an aisle, killing time, idly browsing the
selection of over the counter painkillers.

                    WOMAN'S VOICE (O.S.)
        Robin Ramzinski, come to the pharmacy, your
                prescription's ready.

Randy looks up. He heads down the aisle, toward the
voice. He comes to the Pharmacy counter.

A female PHARMACIST stands holding a small pharmacy bag.

                    PHARMACIST
            Robin Ramzinski?

                    RANDY
            Randy.

                    PHARMACIST
        Just sign here please.

Randy signs the release form. The pharmacist hands
him the bag.

                    PHARMACIST (CONT'D)
        Thank you. Here you go.

EXT. RANDY'S TRAILER - SHORT TIME LATER

Randy hands Len the manager a bunch of cash. Len
counts it.

                    LEN THE MANAGER
            Welcome home.

Len removes the padlock from Randy's trailer door.

            INT. RANDY'S TRAILER - LIVING ROOM -
                    SHORT TIME LATER

Randy sits in the middle of his cramped, junk-filled
trailer.

            INT. RANDY'S TRAILER - LIVING ROOM -
                    SHORT TIME LATER

Tired and sore Randy gingerly closes the living room curtains.

INT. RANDY'S TRAILER - LATER

Randy sleeps in his clothes on the bed, exhausted.

INT. RANDY'S TRAILER - KITCHENETTE - SHORT TIME LATER

Randy examines the various prescriptions he has been given. He swallows his daily dosage.

INT. RANDY'S TRAILER   BEDROOM - SHORT TIME LATER

Randy stands before the mirror examining his wound. His shirt lifted up, he slowly peels back the large SURGERY BANDAGE that covers his chest. A SIX INCH CHEST SCAR runs down the center of his chest, still red and tender.

INT. RANDY'S TRAILER - BATHROOM - LATER

Randy is taking a shower. On his chest is a SURGERY BANDAGE. He soaps up, careful not to get the bandage wet.

CUT TO:

INT. RANDY'S TRAILER - DAY

Randy lies on the couch, reading. Restless. Bored. Something catches his eye.

RANDY'S POV: On the floor, in front of the TV, is an old NINTENDO VIDEOGAME SYSTEM. The game cartridge in the console is WRESTLEJAM '88.

EXT. RANDY'S TRAILER - SHORT TIME LATER

Randy sticks his head out of his trailer.

RANDY'S POV: In front of the opposite trailer, ADAM (8), one of the kids he was play-wrestling with, is idly throwing a tennis ball against a car.

                    RANDY
                 Hey, Adam!

Adam turns and looks toward Randy.

RANDY (CONT'D)
Wanna play Nintendo?

ADAM
Alright.

INT. RANDY'S TRAILER - SHORT TIME LATER

Randy and Adam sit on the floor playing WrestleJam '88.

ON TV:

Cyber-Randy is wrestling The Ayatollah at a packed Madison Square Garden. The graphics are late-'80s crude.

Randy flies all over the ring, devastating his foe with a series of acrobatic leaps and kicks and flips.

RANDY AND ADAM:

Randy wears a look of intense concentration. Adam makes a scrunched-up face at the screen.

RANDY
Okay let's see what you got there.

ADAM
All right. Here comes the Ayatollah.

RANDY
Shaking in my boots. Here we go. Come on.

ADAM
So you hear about Call of Duty Four.

RANDY
Did I what?

ADAM
Call of Duty Four.

RANDY
Call it doodie four?

ADAM
Call Of Duty Four. It's pretty cool.

RANDY
Really?

                    ADAM
                   (sighs)
              This game is **so** old.

                    RANDY
              What's it about?

                    ADAM
It's a war game. Most all the other Call of **Duties**
were based on **World War Two,** but this **one's** with **Iraq.**

                    RANDY
              Oh, yeah?

                    ADAM
And, **yeah, you switch off between** a Marine **and an S
and** S British Special **Operative** so it's pretty cool.

                    RANDY
              Well...

ON **TV:**

Cyber-Randy drops The **Ayatollah** with **a knee** to the
chest. And another. **The Ayatollah GOES DOWN. Randy**
heads to **a** corner **and CLIMBS TO THE** TOP **ROPE.**

                    RANDY (CONT'D)
         Wow. Hold on. All right, hold on.
              There we go.

                    ON **TV:**

He **raises** his arms, **sticking his elbows out,** pressing his fists to **the sides of his** head to form a SET
OF RAM'S HORNS.

Randy JUMPS. He **flies high** in the air, **soaring over**
the mat and **crashing down on** The **Ayatollah** horns-
first. He pins **The Ayatollah as the** ref **counts** to
three for **the victory. The crowd goes wild.**

                    RANDY (CONT'D)
         Ram Jam! You're finished. **Okay,** one **more.**

                    ADAM
              I gotta leave.

                    RANDY
         I just gave you an ass-whipping.
         Don't you wanna get **even?**

                      81

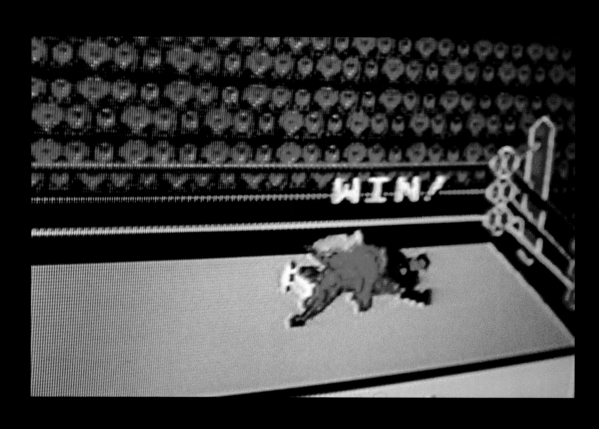

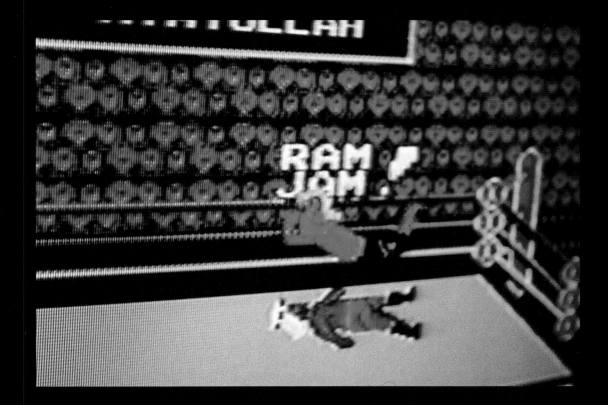

ADAM
Nah, that's okay.

They shake hands.

ADAM(CONT'D)
I'll catch you later all right? See you later man.

RANDY
Do your pushups brother.

ADAM
All right.

Adam gets up and scampers out of the trailer.

EXT. RANDY'S TRAILER - SHORT TIME LATER

Randy, in his sweats does his stretches, preparing for a jog. Hoping to prove the doctor wrong.

EXT. THE WOODS BEHIND RANDY'S TRAILER
- MINUTES LATER

Jogging, he feels himself getting winded. A little woozy. He braces himself against a tree. He crouches down, clutching his chest.

RANDY
Oh fuck.

He sits still, trying to slow his heart.

INT. CHEEQUES- NIGHT

Randy enters the club. It's crowded tonight. He looks around for Cassidy. He spots her in a corner chatting with the other girls.

Randy heads over. Cassidy notices him and gets up.

CASSIDY
Hey! Ram man. Been a while.

She gives him a friendly little cheek peck.

RANDY
Yeah, I was in the neighborhood, thought maybe we could grab a... hamburger.

Cassidy finds the offer a little odd.

This isn't how they operate.

                    CASSIDY
              I'm working.

                    RANDY
                   (nodding)
              Okay. Maybe later?

She looks at him, puzzled. He seems off.

                    CASSIDY
              You okay?

                    RANDY
              Can we talk for a second?

                    CASSIDY
              Sure. What's up? What's up?

                    RANDY
              I mean somewhere quiet.

Randy glances toward the door. Cassidy, catching his
drift, looks at him, a little gravely.

                    CASSIDY
           Randy, I can't leave with a customer you know.

  Pause.

                    RANDY
           Listen, I had a heart attack.

Pause.

                    CASSIDY
              Where you parked?

                    RANDY
              Out in the back.

                    CASSIDY
           Go ahead, go to your car. I'll meet you
              out there in fifteen minutes.

Randy leaves. Cassidy rejoins the girls, but not for
long.

CASSIDY (CONT'D)
(nervously)
You know what, I'm gonna, I'm gonna go on break. I need a cigarette. I can't quit.

EXT. CHEEQUES- REAR PARKING LOT - 5 MINUTES LATER

Randy sits in the van, staring at the club's rear EMERGENCY EXIT. Cassidy emerges, a jacket covering her dress. Randy waves. Spotting him, she comes over, climbing in the passenger side.

RANDY
Thanks. I appreciate it.

CASSIDY
That's okay. When was it?

RANDY
A couple weeks ago.

CASSIDY
Oh. How are you feeling?

RANDY
(chuckles)
I don't feel like Hercules.

CASSIDY
What happened?

RANDY
I was walking in the dressing room and the guys told me I just... dropped like a brick, and you know, I don't remember nothing.
(beat)

Well, now the doctors tell me that I can't... that I can't wrestle no more.

CASSIDY
What are you gonna do?

RANDY
You know, it just don't feel... right. And that's why I wanted to talk to you, you know... 'Cause I don't want to be alone.

Cassidy smiles, a little unnerved.

CASSIDY
Randy...

Randy looks on expectantly.

                    CASSIDY (CONT'D)
        You should be with family now. Don't you have a
          daughter? Where's your daughter?

                         RANDY
            My daughter? She don't like me very much.

                        CASSIDY
          I don't believe it. Everybody needs a father,
        and... trust me, this kind of thing brings people
                  together. You should call her.

Randy nods.

                    CASSIDY (CONT'D)
              I should go back in.
                     (upbeat)
            You gonna be okay huh?

He nods, putting his brave face back on.

                         RANDY
                    I'll be ok.

                        CASSIDY
                         Okay.

Cassidy climbs out of the van. Randy watches as
she heads back into the club. His cheery expression
fades.

                         RANDY
                    (to himself)
                    Stephanie.

                       CUT TO:

INT. RANDY'S TRAILER - NIGHT

Randy sits on his bed, sifting through a messy, junk-
filled shoebox. He pulls out an OLD PHOTO.

RANDY'S POV: It's a mid-'80s school photo of Randy's
daughter STEPHANIE as an 8 year old.

He flips the photo over. On the back are a bunch of
scribbled PHONE NUMBERS. They're all crossed-out ex-
cept the last one. The numbers get progressively more

faded from bottom to top, as if they've been written down over the course of years.

EXT. PARADISE OAKS - PAY PHONE - SHORT TIME LATER

Randy stands at a PAY PHONE with the photo, ringing phone cradled to his ear.

> STEPHANIE'S VOICE
> This is Stephanie, you know what to do.
> *(answering machine BEEP)*

Randy listens to the silence. He hangs up.

INT. VAN - LATER

Randy sits in his van by the curb of a modest, lower middle-class house. He looks at the house, working up the nerve to approach.

EXT. STEPHANIE'S HOUSE - LATER

Randy stands at the doorstep of the house. Steeling himself, he rings the bell. A WOMAN (22) appears at the door in a T-SHIRT and PANTIES.

> RANDY
> *(a little thrown)*
> Hey... Is Stephanie home?

The woman looks at Randy a little coldly, sensing who he is.

                    THE WOMAN
              Who can I say it is?

                      RANDY
               Tell her it's her father.

She disappears into the house.

A few moments later, Stephanie emerges with a BACK-
PACK slung over her shoulder. In her hands is a TEXT-
BOOK. She heads straight down the driveway, blowing
past Randy.

                 RANDY (CONT'D)
            Hey Stephanie! Where you going?

He goes after her.

                        STEPHANIE
                    What do you want?

                         RANDY
              I just... I have to talk to you.

                        STEPHANIE
                 Can't really talk right now.

She resumes walking, briskly.

                         RANDY
                    (chasing after her)
              I really need to talk to you.

                        STEPHANIE
                      I have school.

                         RANDY
            You're going to school? Well, that's great.

He runs to get ahead of her.

                     RANDY (CONT'D)
         Listen. I had a heart attack and I just thought I
                   needed to tell you.

Stephanie is taken aback. She stops and looks at him.

                        STEPHANIE
                 You are such an asshole.

Randy is stunned.

                   STEPHANIE (CONT'D)
         What do you want from me? What do you want?

                         RANDY
         I've just been alone and you're my daughter and I
              love you and I just needed to see you.

                        STEPHANIE
         That's bullshit. You want me to take care of you.

Randy shakes his head.

                   STEPHANIE (CONT'D)
         Yes. Well, I'm not gonna do that. 'Cause where the
         fuck were you when I needed you to take care of me?

Randy has no answer. Stephanie is distraught.

STEPHANIE (CONT'D)
You know on **all my** birthdays, which you **never** even
made one. **You** probably don't even know when it is!
So **you know what?** No. I don't care if **you** had a
heart attack. Fuck you!

Stephanie walks off. Randy watches her stunned.

CUT TO:

EXT. RAHWAY AMERICAN LEGION - HALL - AFTERNOON

Randy enters, duffle bag over his shoulder.

INT. RAHWAY AMERICAN LEGION - GYMNASIUM - MORNING

Randy walks into the meeting hall. In the center of
the room there are a FEW FOLDING TABLES set up. At
each one a BEAT-UP, WORN-OUT WRESTLER lays out his
wares and memorabilia.

Randy is greeted by Scott Brumberg, the promoter from
the opening scene. He's wearing the same "BRUMBERG
- 44" Mets jersey.

SCOTT BRUMBERG
Ram!

RANDY
Hey.

SCOTT BRUMBERG
Didn't think I'd see you here.

RANDY
Why not?

SCOTT BRUMBERG
I heard you collapsed at the DiFusco show.

RANDY
Man, I just overheated and blacked out. That's all.

SCOTT BRUMBERG
Really?

RANDY
Yeah, I was out of the hospital in less than an hour.

SCOTT BRUMBERG
So you're fine?

                              RANDY
                    Brother I'm good to go.

                        SCOTT BRUMBERG
                          (chuckling)
                    Well, that's excellent!
             I was just gonna cancel the minivan.

Randy looks at him, surprised.

                              RANDY
                         What minivan?

                        SCOTT BRUMBERG
           I rented one for fanfest. Me and the whole gang's
          driving down. Terry C. Caggiano, Fatback... I'm so
                         fucking psyched!

Randy looks at him blankly.

                              RANDY
                              Oh.

                        SCOTT BRUMBERG
             Volpe gave me an assload of fliers.

Brumberg hands Randy a BRIGHT-ORANGE FLIER from a
stack on a nearby table.

                    SCOTT BRUMBERG (CONT'D)
                             Here.

RANDY'S POV: The flier.

                    RING OF HONOR PRESENTS
              **** "LEGENDS OF THE RING" FANFEST ****
                         April 3, 2009

        WILMINGTON RIALTO THEATER - WILMINGTON, DELAWARE

        THE MAIN EVENT... IN A 20TH ANNIVERSARY REMATCH OF
        THEIR LEGENDERY EPIC April 1, 1989 WRESTLESLAM IV
                            MATCH...

          RANDY "THE RAM" ROBINSON VS. THE AYATOLLAH

                  ALSO SCHEDULED TO APPEAR:
        EDDIE RUCKUS, THE MORTICIAN, DEAN "THE DREAM" GI-
        GUNDA, IVAN PETROV, THE SANDBAGGERS, BILLY BOB
        BANJO, J.T. SEXXY, CORPORAL PUNISHMENT, CHRIS CO-
                    LUMBO...AND MANY MORE!

Randy nods vaguely at the flyer, his feelings hard to read.

> SCOTT BRUMBERG (CONT'D)
> It's gonna be epic. Volpe said that the scout from the show was gonna be there. Randy stares at the flier, torn.

> SCOTT BRUMBERG (CONT'D)
> Twenty years in the making

> RANDY
> It's gonna be something.

> SCOTT BRUMBERG
> Yeah, come on, I got you set up down there.

Scott leads Randy to his table on the other side of the room

> SCOTT BRUMBERG (CONT'D)
> So, yeah, should get a pretty good crowd tonight.

Randy holds up his hand, wiggling his fingers for Brumberg.

> RANDY
> Great, I'll loosen up.

Scott leaves. An AGING WRESTLER calls out to Randy.

> AGING WRESTLER
> **Ram!**

> RANDY
> Hey my man, how you doing big guy? Good to see you.

They hug

> AGING WRESTLER
> I haven't seen you in a while.

INT. RAHWAY AMERICAN LEGION - HALL - MINUTES LATER

Randy arranges his memorabilia on the folding table in front of him. He pulls out a stack of t-shirts that have his heroic image and logo on them and places them neatly next to a stack of fliers for the Ayatollah rematch show.

He takes out a stack of his VHS tapes and a Polaroid camera.

As he finishes setting up, he takes a moment to look at the flier.

INT. GYMNASIUM - SHORT TIME LATER

The signing is underway. FIVE OR SO FANS mill about the room, drifting from table to table getting auto-graphs and taking photos with the motley assortment of washed-up aging wrestlers.

                    FAN
          Hey, Ram. Been a big fan of yours for
          years. It's really great to meet you.

                    RANDY
          Hey. How you doing brother?

                    FAN
          Can I get a polaroid?

Brumberg takes their picture. Randy signs the polaroid.

A mother and son ask to have their picture taken with Randy as well. Brumberg again acts as the cameraman.

                    SCOTT BRUMBERG
                  (snapping the photo)
              One! Two! Ram!

                    RANDY
          There you go. That's eight.

The mother hands Randy 8 DOLLARS and he tucks it into the FANNY PACK he's wearing.

INT. GYMNASIUM - SHORT TIME LATER

Randy sits at his table, bored. There are NO TAKERS. He looks around the room at the other wrestlers.

RANDY'S POV: One is asleep. Another looks borderline homeless.

Across from him is a 40-SOMETHING WRESTLER in a WHEELCHAIR. Attached to his calf is a URINE BAG. A feeble stream of urine trickles into the bag.

Randy considers this sad tableaux.

CUT TO:

INT. CHEEQUES- **SHORT TIME LATER**

MUSIC — DEESHA SARAI feat. CRITICAL CHILD
— "JUST LET YOUR FREAK OUT"

Cassidy approaches a customer.

> CASSIDY
> Hi, I'm Cassidy.

> HENRY
> Henry,

> CASSIDY
> Nice to meet you. Where you from?

> HENRY
> Garfield.

> CASSIDY
> **Yeah? How you doing tonight?**

> HENRY
> Okay.

> CASSIDY
> How about a private dance,
> make you feel a little better?

> HENRY
> (considering)
> No, not tonight.

> CASSIDY
> **No, Henry?**

> HENRY
> No.

> CASSIDY
> (disappointed)
> **No? Okay.**

INT. CHEEQUES - SHORT TIME LATER

MUSIC: TRAI'D - "Hit Da Flo"

She approaches a PAIR OF GUYS. She leans in to one
of them. They look at her and decline as well.

101

Cassidy heads off, rejected.

                    RANDY (O.S.)
                    Hey. Hey you.

She turns and sees Randy at the bar. She's happy to
see him after the string of no's.

                    CASSIDY
                    Hi. When'd you get here?

                    RANDY
                    I just flew in.

She sits down at the bar next to him.

                    CASSIDY
                    You did? How you been feeling?

                    RANDY
                    I'm feeling good. Feeling a lot better.

                    CASSIDY
                    Good.

                    RANDY
                    And I took your advice.
                    I went and saw my daughter.

                    CASSIDY
                    Yeah?

                    RANDY
                    Yeah.

                    CASSIDY
                    How did that go?

                    RANDY
            It didn't go very well... She sort of... ripped me
                    a new asshole.

                    CASSIDY
                    Oh, no, sorry to hear that.

                    RANDY
        Well, hey, what are you gonna do? You know... maybe
        if I went out and did something special, you know?
        Bought her a present? I was thinking about maybe
                    getting her a present.

                              CASSIDY
                    That's a really great idea!
                              (beat)
                         What's she into?

          Randy looks at her blankly.

                               RANDY
                         I don't really...

                              CASSIDY
                  What kind of music does she like?

                               RANDY
                        I really don't know.

                              CASSIDY
           Well, is she into something else, like, I don't
               know, cooking or books or something?

          Again Randy comes up with nothing.

                               RANDY
                              (sighs)
                        Oh. I don't know.

                              CASSIDY
             Okay. Well, you should get her clothes, some kind
                  of clothes. All girls like that.

                               RANDY
                               Yeah?

                              CASSIDY
                               Yeah.

          Struck with the urge to help Cassidy grabs a napkin
          and a pen off the bar.

                          CASSIDY (CONT'D)
             Hey, I know the right place. It's this kick-ass
                  little vintage shop in Elizabeth.

          She scribbles down VINTAGE MODE - ELIZABETH. Hands
          it to him.

                          CASSIDY (CONT'D)
              I think it's on Elizabeth Avenue. You should go
              Saturday. That's when they get all the best shit.

          Randy is genuinely thankful.

                              RANDY
                       Hey thanks. Thanks a lot.

There is a brief lull in the conversation. Cassidy
touches his hand.

                             CASSIDY
                           Want a dance?

                              RANDY
               Uh... I don't think I'm quite ready for that yet.

Cassidy gets up, rejected by another patron. CAMERA
stays on her as she walks around the club looking for
customers.

She scans the room. She sees yet another potential
CUSTOMER. She looks back toward Randy again. He's
sitting at the bar alone. She heads over to him.

He looks up from his drink.

                          RANDY (CONT'D)
                        Well, that was fast.

                             CASSIDY
          Listen, why don't I meet you there Saturday? Help
                     you picking something out.

                              RANDY
                      Wow, I'd like that a lot.

                             CASSIDY
                              One?

                              RANDY
                              Yeah.

                             CASSIDY
                           All right.

She gives him a chummy look and walks off.

                              RANDY
                          (to himself)
                        One o'clock. One.

                      EXT. ACME - MORNING

Randy walks across the parking lot towards the Acme
supermarket.

INT. ACME - MORNING

Randy opens the **door** to Wayne's office.

>   RANDY
>   Hey. Whoa.

Randy stops. Wayne is looking at porn on his computer.

>   WAYNE
>   Did you forget how to knock?

>   RANDY
>   No.

>   WAYNE
>   (*waving him away*)
>   Let's try that **again**. I'm serious.

Randy steps out and closes the **door** behind him. He knocks.

Wayne opens the door abruptly, hitting Randy full-on. He shoots past him, irked.

>   WAYNE (CONT'D)
>   **What** do you want?

>   RANDY
>   Well, I was wondering if I could get some more work.
>   Something steady. Full-time.

>   WAYNE
>   (*remembering to himself*)
>   Cellphone.

He turns back towards his office.

>   WAYNE (CONT'D)
>   All I got is weekends.

>   RANDY
>   Yeah, well, that works.

>   WAYNE
>   Isn't that when you sit on other dudes' faces?

>   RANDY
>   So what do you got?

                          WAYNE
                      Deli counter.

Randy seems a little hesitant.

                          RANDY
         Deli counter. Dealing with the customers and stuff?

                          WAYNE
         Yeah. A parade of hot, horny housewives begging for
                         your meat.

Randy thinks it over.

                          RANDY
                   You got anything else?

                          WAYNE
                No I do not. Interested?

                          RANDY
                      (resignedly)
                     Yeah, sure.

              EXT. VINTAGE NODE - DAY

Randy stands alone in front of a vintage clothing
store. Cassidy pulls up in her 80s PICKUP TRUCK.
Randy is all smiles.

                          RANDY
                         Hey.

                         CASSIDY
                         Hey.

RANDY'S POV: It's his first time seeing Cassidy in
street clothes and in daylight. She's not wearing
makeup, and her hair is pulled back in a ponytail.
She's also a good three inches shorter out of her
stripper heels.

                          RANDY
         Goddamn, I almost didn't recognize you. You look
                   all... you look clean.

                         CASSIDY
                        "Clean"?

                          RANDY
              No, I mean you look lovely.

                              CASSIDY
                          Ok... thanks.

                              RANDY
            Uh, listen, should I call you, uh, Pam or Cassidy
                           or what?

She gives the question genuine thought.

                              CASSIDY
                               Pam.
                             (playful)
                       Don't get used to it.

            INT. VINTAGE MODE - SHORT TIME LATER

Randy follows Cassidy toward the back of the store. He
looks around, taking in the array of funky '50s/'60s/
'70s clothes.

                              CASSIDY
              So like, what is she? Goth? Punk? Hippie?
                              (beat)
                             Preppy?

Randy ponders the choices.

                              RANDY
                Oh, yeah, I ain't got a clue...

Randy watches as she continues searching.

                         RANDY (CONT'D)
                           Hey, Pam?

                              CASSIDY
                              Yeah?

                              RANDY
                  Thank you. I really appreciate this.

Cassidy looks at him. She can feel his sincere appre-
ciation.

                              CASSIDY
                          You're welcome.

She returns to searching. Sift, sift, sift, sift...

                              RANDY
              Uh, listen... I think Stephanie is a... a lesbian.

Cassidy stops sifting. She looks up at him.

                    CASSIDY
                    Uh-huh?

                    RANDY
              (motioning to the clothes)
          Does that make a difference what she...

                    CASSIDY
               No. It's cool.

                    RANDY
    I mean, or maybe it's all in my head. I don't know.

Randy starts sifting through the racks. He finds a
shiny green ROLLER-DISCO JACKET with a big embroi-
dered S over the left breast. It's UGLY.

                    RANDY (CONT'D)
                    (excited)
    Oh, wow, what about this? Look at this, it's got an
    "S" on it.

Cassidy clearly find it hideous, but keeps it to herself.

                    RANDY (CONT'D)
               It's perfect, huh?

                    CASSIDY
        Well, I mean, it's winter, so maybe you'll want
                 something warmer...

Cassidy's eyes drift toward a rack of coats. She
grabs a NAVY PEA COAT.

                    CASSIDY (CONT'D)
                ...like a pea coat.

Randy admires her choice

                    RANDY
               You got a point there.

                    CASSIDY
            I don't know her size.

                    RANDY
          Yeah, that's pretty cool.

He turns his attention back to the DISCO JACKET.

                    RANDY (CONT'D)
        I don't know, man. I think that's pretty rock-and-
              roll... what do you think?

Cassidy looks at Randy who's beaming with excitement
and pride. She finds it endearing.

                    CASSIDY
        I... you should go with your gut, man.

                    RANDY
                    Yeah?

                    CASSIDY
                    Yeah.

            EXT. VINTAGE MODE - LATER

Cassidy and Randy exit the store.

                    RANDY
        You look so goddamn pretty in the daytime.

Cassidy is flattered.

                    RANDY (CONT'D)
        Hey, you have a beer with me?

                    CASSIDY
            Uh, I gotta get going.

                    RANDY
            One beer.

Cassidy seems torn.

                    CASSIDY
            I really...
                    (beat)
        I got a... I got a kid.

                    RANDY
        You have a kid?

Cassidy nods. Yup.

                    RANDY (CONT'D)
        Well. What do you have a boy or a girl?

                    CASSIDY
            Boy. Jameson.

                    RANDY
               How old?

                   CASSIDY
                   Nine.

                    RANDY
            Wow. Who would figure, huh?

                   CASSIDY
     It's not something I usually tell customers. It's
          not exactly... it's not a turn-on.

An idea hits Randy.

                    RANDY
          Ah, hold on. Wait a second.

Randy jogs to his van parked by the curb. Cassidy
watches him go, not sure what he's doing. A moment
later he returns with THE RANDY THE RAM ACTION FIGURE
FROM THE DASHBOARD. He proudly, excitedly holds it
out to Cassidy.

               RANDY (CONT'D)
     I want you to give this to your little guy. It's a
          Randy the Ram action figure.

She looks at the action figure, laughs.

               RANDY (CONT'D)
     Tell him not to lose it. It's a three hundred dol-
          lar collector's item.

She takes it.

                   CASSIDY
                  Really?

                    RANDY
                    Nah.

Cassidy laughs a little. She can't help but be charmed
by his sweetness and earnestness. After a pause...

               RANDY (CONT'D)
          C'mon, hey, one beer.

                   CASSIDY
                   Okay.

INT. FRENCHY'S - SHORT TIME LATER

Randy holds Cassidy's CELLPHONE, he's looking at
PICTURES of her son.

                    RANDY
          Great-lookin' kid you got there.

Cassidy and Randy are having beers at a bar. Cassidy
proudly smiles.

                    CASSIDY
               I think so.

                    RANDY
          Well, I can see where he got his good looks from.

Cassidy smiles, flattered.

                    CASSIDY
          Yeah, well, he doesn't get it from his father.

Randy skips to the next pic. It's a shot of an UNDER
CONSTRUCTION CONDO BUILDING.

                    RANDY
               What's that?

                    CASSIDY
          Oh, that's this condo thing, down by Tampa.

                    RANDY
          What, are you thinking about moving there?

                    CASSIDY
               Working on it. Yeah.

                    RANDY
               Yeah?

                    CASSIDY
          Mm-hm. Yeah, the schools are really awesome. Great
               neighborhood, and...cheaper.

                    RANDY
          What about your gig over at Cheeques?

                    CASSIDY
               Done. Quitting.

                            RANDY
                    (a little disappointed)
                        Oh, wow...

A new song comes on over the jukebox.

                MUSIC: RATT ATTACK - "ROUND AND ROUND"

Randy's ears perk up at the song on the jukebox. He
starts to dance.

                        RANDY (CONT'D)
                Woah, hell, yeah.

He stands up, reaching out for Cassidy's hand. She
doesn't give it.

                        RANDY (CONT'D)
            Come on baby. Dance with me. Come on.

                            CASSIDY
                          (laughs)
                        Here?

                            RANDY
            Yeah, right here. Come on.

                            CASSIDY
                        (chuckles)
                No, I've danced to this plenty.

                            RANDY
        Okay, I'll dance for you then. Okay here we go.

Randy starts DANCING in front of Cassidy, who's sitting
on a barstool. She smiles.

                            CASSIDY
                I think I can get you a shift.

                            RANDY
                Hey, man, I need a job.

Cassidy breaks out in laughter.

                        RANDY (CONT'D)
                        There we go.

Randy moves in, starts to dance between her legs.

                        CASSIDY
            Is this a lapdance I'm getting?

Randy **starts** singing **along with** the song.

                        RANDY
        'I **knew** right from **the** beginning'

Cassidy, unable to **resist** the song joins in, Randy
still dancing between **her** legs, unembarrassed.

                    CASSIDY & RANDY
    'that you would end **up** winning / I knew **right from**
    the start / you'd **put** an arrow through my **heart** /
                    round **and** round'

They **laugh together.** They stop **to take a** drink.

                        RANDY
        Goddamn **they** don't make em like **they** used to.

                        CASSIDY
        Fucking **Eighties** man. **Best shit ever.**

                        RANDY
        Bet **your** ass man. Guns'**N'Roses** fucking **rules.**

                        CASSIDY
                        Crüe...

                        RANDY
                        Yeah.

                        CASSIDY
                        Def lep.

                        RANDY
        Then that Cobain **pussy had** to **come** around and ruin
                    it all, **you know?**

                        CASSIDY
        Like there's **something wrong with** wanting to have a
                        good time.

                        RANDY
                Now I'll tell **you** something,
                I hated **the** fucking **Nineties.**

                        CASSIDY
                        (laughs)
                Nineties fucking sucked.

                              RANDY
                      Nineties fuckin' sucked.

Nodding, Randy leans in and KISSES Cassidy. She pulls
away, looks into his eyes, then KISSES BACK. They
MAKE OUT for a few seconds. Cassidy PULLS BACK.

                             CASSIDY
                           Shit. Fuck.

                              RANDY
                      What's the matter?

She playfully smacks herself in the face, masking her
fear and discomfort with what just happened.

                             CASSIDY
               No contact with the customers. I gotta go.

She turns to leave. Randy is confused.

                              RANDY
                      You said one beer.

She turns back.

                             .CASSIDY
                             I did?

                              RANDY
                             Yeah.

                             .CASSIDY
                           Oh, okay.

Cassidy picks up her ALMOST FULL BEER and CHUGS the
whole thing. She slaps the empty bottle on the bar.

                        CASSIDY (CONT'D)
                            (sighing)
                          One beer.

She collects her things and leaves. Randy looks after
her, impressed.

           INT. ACME - EMPLOYEE ROOM - MORNING

It's Randy's first day of work He slips into a DELI
COAT. He stands in front of a mirror, and tucks his
hair into a hairnet. He feels a little silly.

                    WAYNE (O.S.)
              Here ya go. Right here.

He turns and sees Wayne, who hands him something. Randy
looks at the item in his hand, vaguely bothered.

                    RANDY
        Hey bro, this is supposed to say 'Randy'.

ANGLE ON item, a ACME NAME TAG. The name on it is
ROBIN.

                    WAYNE
         I guess they got it off your W-4.

                    RANDY
        So I really gotta wear one of these things?

                    WAYNE
                 (sarcastic)
             No, you're special.

                    RANDY
         Well, uh, can you change it?

                    WAYNE
        Just wear the fucking thing, all right?

Wayne walks off. Randy pins the name tag to his
apron. He takes another look in the mirror, he's
clearly unhappy.

              INT. ACME - CONTINUOUS

We follow behind him as he walks out of the locker
area, down the hallway, past the electrical room,
through the break area, down the stairs to the stor-
age and loading area.

He heads toward a RUBBER-STRIP CURTAIN leading to the
deli counter, Standing before the curtain, he pauses
a moment, gathering himself like before a wrestling
match.

He steps through. Showtime.

            INT. DELI COUNTER - SHORT TIME LATER

Randy rips off some wax paper and wraps up someone's
boloney, He finishes and slaps it down on the counter
for an OLD GUY in a WWII VETERAN baseball cap.

                              RANDY
                     Here's your baloney pal.

He turns and presses the button for the number of the
next person. The L.E.D display reads 18.

                          RANDY (CONT'D)
                           Eighteen!

A WOMAN (60s) steps forward holding an ACME CIRCULAR.
She carefully surveys the TURKEY-BREAST SELECTION in
the case.

                              WOMAN
               Are they all on sale or just the regular ones?

Randy looks clueless.

                              RANDY
                     The Hudson Acres, uh...

                              WOMAN
                       (holding up circular)
                     Well, it wasn't very clear.

                              RANDY
                        Let me check.

Randy picks up the intercom behind the counter.

                          RANDY(CONT'D)
                     Wayne, to the deli counter.
                           (to woman)
                     It'll just be a minute.

                              WOMAN
               Okay... so which in your opinion is the best
                         smoked ham?

Randy is distracted by another customer, a BIG-
HAIRED, SEMI-HOT PARTY CHICK in her forties. The kind
of woman Randy would hit on in a bar.

                              RANDY
                        The best what?

                              WOMAN
                           (annoyed)
                        Smoked ham.

                    RANDY
                    Uh...

                    WOMAN
                    Which?

                    RANDY
                  (grasping)
        Smoked ham... I guess the maple-glazed is not bad.

              INT. DELI COUNTER - LATER

        Randy sprays cooking grease on the rotisserie.

              INT. DELI COUNTER - LATER

        Standing at a large industrial grade deep fryer,
        a female DELI COUNTER WORKER shows him how to fry
        chicken.

                    RANDY
              Breasts, thighs, small pieces.

              DELI COUNTER WORKER
              Breasts, thighs, right.

                    RANDY
              Lock it up. Push start

              DELI COUNTER WORKER
                    Yes.

        Following the lesson, Randy throws the chicken pieces
        in the gurgling grease and starts the machine.

              INT. DELI COUNTER - LATER

        ANGLE ON Take-A-Number sign. It says NOW SERVING: 46.

                    RANDY
                 Forty-six.

        A WOMAN (35) in workout clothes steps forward with
        a 46.

                 WORKOUT WOMAN
        Could I get a half-pound of pesto pasta salad?

                    RANDY
                Okay, coming up.

The Le___
(95% to 98% Fat Free)

NO MONOSODIUM GLUTAMATE

NOW SERVING

TURN-O-MATIC

Randy scoops pesto pasta salad into the container. He
puts the container onto the scale. It reads .51 LB.

>   RANDY (CONT'D)
>   Half a pound of pesto pasta salad on the button.

This gets Randy a small chuckle from the woman. Randy
slaps a price tag on the container.

>   RANDY (CONT'D)
>   Can I get you anything else?

>   YOUNG WOMAN
>   No, that's it.

He hands her the container.

>   RANDY
>   You have a lovely day, darling.

>   YOUNG WOMAN
>   (friendly smile)
>   Thanks. You too.

The woman heads off. Randy's spirits are lifted by
the .exchange. He turns back to the Take-A-Number
sign. Presses the button.

>   RANDY
>   Forty-seven!

INT. DELI COUNTER - LATER

Randy slices deli meat. A FEMALE CUSTOMER (40) stands
at the counter.

>   FEMALE CUSTOMER
>   Let me get a eight-piece, uh, chicken.

>   RANDY
>   What kind of chicken you want?

>   FEMALE CUSTOMER
>   I want a eight-piece. That's two breasts.
>   Give me two big breasts.

>   RANDY
>   Two big breasts, coming up.

He starts to pick out chicken.

                    RANDY (CONT'D)
                      (joking)
        That's what I want, two big breasts.

The female customer laughs.

                    RANDY (CONT'D)
        Two big breasts, and, uh. something with
                      a brain.

Randy leans in to pick out more chicken.

                    RANDY (CONT'D)
                  And two wings?
        Yeah, stay away from those thighs.

He finishes wrapping up the chicken and hands it to her.

                    RANDY (CONT'D)
        A lot of chicken flying out the door. There you go,
                honey. Have a good day.

The female customer smiles, thanking him. Randy
smiles, he's starting to enjoy this.

                    RANDY (CONT'D)
                   Who's next?

A MALE CUSTOMER (40) approaches the counter.

                    RANDY (CONT'D)
        What you having good looking?

                    MALE CUSTOMER
        Uh, half a pound of egg salad.

                      RANDY
        Half a pound of egg salad, coming up.

Randy heads over to the appropriate section of the
display case, on his way he playfully THROWS AN
ELBOW at a nearby pole adding his own sound effect.
He opens the case and dishes out some egg salad into
a container.

                    MALE CUSTOMER
                   Is it fresh?

                      RANDY
        Fresh? Fresh as monkey's breath brother!
              This is the good stuff.

He finishes scooping. He starts motioning to the customer to catch the container as if it were a football.

                    RANDY (CONT'D)
Coming up. Down and out, come on. It's the fourth
quarter. Come on, come on, come on. There's twelve
seconds left. Go. Down and out, here. Both hands.

The customer reluctantly takes a few steps back.
Randy throws the container, the man catches it in his
shopping basket.

                    RANDY (CONT'D)
Hey! Touchdown! Goddamn! How about them Cowboys?

Randy, living it up, heads over to the next customer,
an ELDERLY WOMAN (80).

                    RANDY (CONT'D)
What you having, spring chicken?

                    CUT TO:

EXT. MIELEVILLE - PAY PHONE - DAY

Randy stands at the pay phone. In his hands is his
day planner open to a page marked up with upcoming
gigs. He makes a call.

                    RANDY
          Hey, Migg, how you doing?

                    MIGG
               Who's this?

                    RANDY
          Yeah, it's the Ram.

                    MIGG
     Hey, Ram, good to hear from you.
     We gonna see you in two weeks?

                    RANDY
          Yeah, sure, yeah.

                    MIGG
     It's gonna be big. I got twelve calls already.

                    RANDY
     Yeah. Listen, uh, you're gonna have to count me out
               of Utica.

                    126

                              MIGG
              What do you mean? We've been selling
                    tickets for a week!

                              RANDY
                     Well, I'm retiring.

EXT. PAY PHONE - MOMENTS LATER

Another call.

                              RANDY
                  Hey, Frank, how you doing?

                              FRANK
              Yeah, good, Ram, good. How are you?

                              RANDY
              I'm good, man, I'm good. Uh, listen....

     EXT. PAY PHONE - MOMENTS LATER

Another call. Randy is holding the Fanfest flyer.

                              RANDY
              Ah, come on, I'm sorry, Volpe, you know
                    I'd kill to do it.

                           NICK VOLPE
                  Ram. I already bought Bob's plane
                  ticket. Do you know how much...

                              RANDY
                  No, I realize, I understand.

                           NICK VOLPE
              I think you're making a big mistake.

                              RANDY
                  No more. I am done. I'm retired.

                           NICK VOLPE
                       Yeah, I know.

Randy hangs up. He sighs, looking at the flyer.

                       INT. BUS - DAY

Stephanie is riding a New Jersey Transit bus. The bus
slows. She gets off.

EXT. STEPHANIE'S STREET - SHORT TIME LATER

Stephanie is walking down her block. She is surprised to see, parked in front of her house, Randy's van. He jumps out. Tucked under his arm is a LUMPILY WRAPPED PRESENT.

                    STEPHANIE
          What are you, stalking me?

                    RANDY
          No, I... brought you a present.

He excitedly hands her the gift. She looks at it warily.

                    RANDY (CONT'D)
          Go ahead. Open it.

She opens it. Inside is the green satin jacket. She holds it up, trying to process.

                    RANDY (CONT'D)
          The "S" is for "Stephanie".

                    STEPHANIE
          Oh. Yeah.

She looks at the jacket, a little bewildered. It's nothing she'd ever wear.

                    RANDY
          Do you like it?

                    STEPHANIE
          It's... shiny.

Randy can tell she doesn't like it.

                    RANDY
          That's not really your present,
          I got you something else. Hold on.

He reaches back into the van and pulls out ANOTHER WRAPPED GIFT.

                    RANDY (CONT'D)
              (hands her the second gift)
          This is the real present.

Stephanie unwraps it.

                    STEPHANIE
                 It's a pea coat.

She holds it up, giving in a bit.

                      RANDY
                Yeah. Well, it's wintertime,
                and I want you to keep warm.

                    STEPHANIE
                (eye contact, touched)
                 Thank you.

                      RANDY
                Anything for you sweetheart.

A tentative pause between them.

                    RANDY (CONT'D)
                 So what are you doing right now?

                    STEPHANIE
                 What am I doing?

                      RANDY
        I thought maybe we could stop by our old favorite
                          place.

                    STEPHANIE
                 We have an old favorite spot?

                      RANDY
                You'll recognize it when you see it.

                    STEPHANIE
                Now's not really the best time.
                I've got something I gotta do.

                      RANDY
                 What kinda stuff?

                    STEPHANIE
                 Just... stuff.

He gives her his biggest, most charming puppy-dog
smile.

                      RANDY
        C'mon, I'm not gonna take a bite out of you or
        anything, just, you know, hang out for a little
                          while.

Stephanie looks back at him, torn, remembering old wounds.

EXT. ASBURY PARK BOARDWALK - LATER

Randy and Stephanie walk along the boardwalk. It's a bit cold and abandoned.

                    STEPHANIE
               (looks around, marveling)
          I haven't been here in ages.

                    RANDY
          You remember the funhouse?

Randy points towards a spot down the way.

                    RANDY (CONT'D)
          Right there. It used to be The Monster Motel.

                    STEPHANIE
               (unsure)
          Uh, kind of.

                    RANDY
          You loved it. We used to go in there and they had
          this spooky-ass skeleton, it would pop out of a
          coffin. You'd get really scared and cry and wanna
          run out. And then you'd beg to go back in again.

                    STEPHANIE
               (chuckles to self)
          Always was a glutton for punishment.

                    RANDY
          Yeah. You wouldn't go in unless you could sit on
          my foot and wrap your arms around my leg. And we'd
          walk all the way through like that.

                    STEPHANIE
          I don't even remember that.

                    RANDY
               (looks at her sweetly)
          I do.

EXT. BOARDWALK - SHORT TIME LATER

Randy and Stephanie face one another, straddling a
large window ledge. Randy is quiet and contemplative,

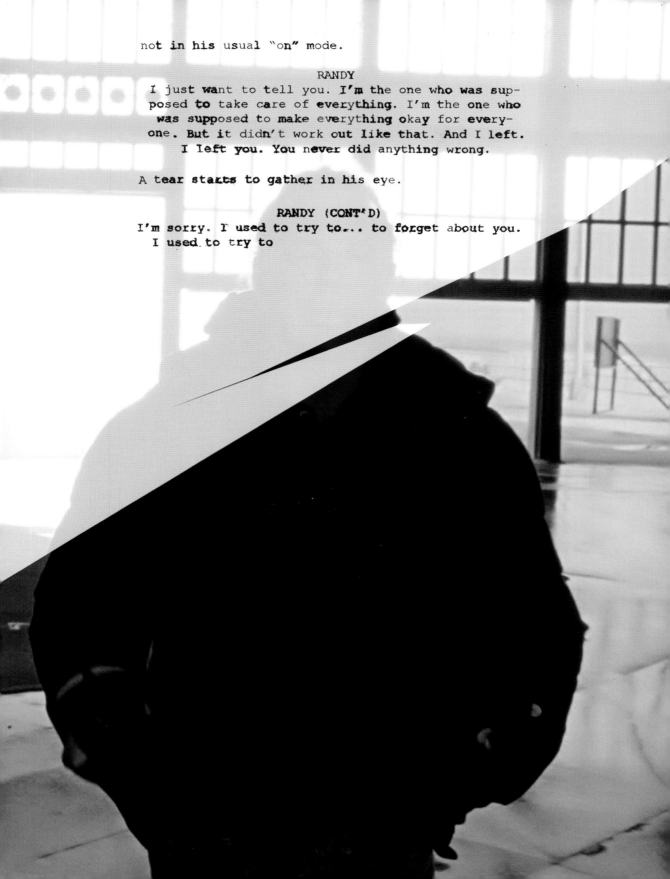

not in his usual "on" mode.

                        RANDY
        I just want to tell you. I'm the one who was sup-
        posed to take care of everything. I'm the one who
        was supposed to make everything okay for every-
        one. But it didn't work out like that. And I left.
        I left you. You never did anything wrong.

A tear starts to gather in his eye.

                   RANDY (CONT'D)
    I'm sorry. I used to try to... to forget about you.
        I used to try to

                         pretend that you didn't exist.
                         But I can't.
                                  (beat)
                    You're my girl. You're my little...

Randy chokes up.

                         RANDY (CONT'D)
                    You're my little girl. And now I'm an old, broken-
                    down piece of meat. And I'm alone. And I deserve
                    to be all alone. I just don't want you to hate me.
                                  Okay?

Stephanie nods, moved.

                    INT. CASINO ATRIUM - SHORT TIME LATER

Randy and Stephanie walk into an old run down CASINO
ATRIUM. As they walk, Stephanie puts her arm around
Randy's and leans her head on his shoulder.

As they walk deeper into the hall, Stephanie notices
a PADLOCKED DOOR. She separates from Randy and goes
over to the door to peek through a hole. She is excited by what she sees and KICKS THE DOOR IN, and
beckons Randy to follow her inside.

                              RANDY
                    Oh, man, we can't go in there.

                             STEPHANIE
                              Come on.

He follows her into the once beautiful heart of the
casino, a large crumbling ballroom.

                         STEPHANIE(CONT'D)
                              Oh my god.

                    RANDY
               Oh man. Wow.

                  STEPHANIE
Wow, this must have been a ballroom or something.

                    RANDY
Oh, look at this. We can... hey, here we go.

Randy bows, extending his hand, asking as properly as
he can, for a dance.

                  STEPHANIE
               What is that?

                    RANDY
            It's my bow to you.

            He bows again.

                  STEPHANIE
Am I supposed to bow back? I bow to you?

Stephanie bows, mirroring his gesture. They begin to
waltz.

            STEPHANIE (CONT'D)
       You can lead. You're not bad.

                    RANDY
                 (beaming)
               Thank you.

EXT. STEPHANIE'S HOUSE - SHORT TIME LATER

Randy and Stephanie park in front of her house.

                    RANDY
      Hold on. Wait, let me get the door.

Acting the part of a gentleman, he runs around to
open her door, They get out and stand in front of her
house, about to part ways.

                 RANDY (CONT'D)
   Well, I hope that wasn't too painful for you.

                  STEPHANIE
            No, it was okay.

                        RANDY
                Well, okay... bye.

                      STEPHANIE
                        Bye.

Stephanie starts to walk to the door.

                        RANDY
        Hey, maybe we could go out to dinner sometime?

                      STEPHANIE
                       Dinner?

                        RANDY
                On Friday or something?

Stephanie thinks it over.

                    RANDY (CONT'D)
                 (nodding, "casual")
                Whatever works for you.

                      STEPHANIE
                Saturday would be better.

                        RANDY
                       Saturday?

                      STEPHANIE
                        Yeah.

                        RANDY
                      You got it.

Randy is surprised and happy. Stephanie turns and
smiles goodbye before entering her house.

            INT. RANDY'S TRAILER - LATER

Randy sticks the old school photo of Stephanie on the
fridge. He steps back and swigs a beer, pleased with
himself.

            INT. CHEEQUES- NIGHT

        MUSIC: SLAUGHTER - "DANGEROUS"

Cassidy is up on stage, doing her thing for a size-
able crowd. She slinks up to a customer who's holding
out a dollar bill for her. She pulls on her G-string

                         136

band, snapping it shut on the bill. She moves over to another customer holding out a dollar and does the same.

                    RANDY (O.S.)
                  Hey. Over here.

She looks toward the voice, coming from another side of the stage.

CASSIDY'S POV: Standing there is Randy, holding out a PURPLE ENVELOPE. He looks toward her G-string, like he wants to put it in like a dollar bill. She takes it with her hand instead.

          INT. CHEEQUES- SHORT TIME LATER

Randy and Cassidy sit together at a table. Cassidy is holding the purple envelope, looking a little uncomfortable.

                    RANDY
                  Come on, open it.

                    CASSIDY
            I'll wait till later when it's quiet.

                    RANDY
                  Come on.
            I want to watch your face when you read it.

Reluctantly, Cassidy opens it. Inside is a GREETING CARD.

CASSIDY'S POV: On the card's front, a cartoon monkey is holding a big bunch of bananas. Across the top it says THANKS A BUNCH!

Randy watches excitedly as she reads the inside. She puts it down after reading it.

                    CASSIDY
            Thank you. That's very sweet.

                    RANDY
            Hey, thank you. I mean, come on, baby,
                  you saved my ass.

He reaches out for her hand. She pulls it away. He looks at her confused.

                    RANDY (CONT'D)
                    What?

                    CASSIDY
                    I can't do this.

                    RANDY
                    You can't do what?

                    CASSIDY
                    ("you and me" gesture)
                    This.

Randy is confused and disappointed.

                    RANDY
I thought we had a little something going here.

                    CASSIDY
            No, well...I think you're awesome.
                    You're a great guy.

                    RANDY
            So what's the problem.

                    CASSIDY
You think I'm, like, this stripper, and I'm not. I
have responsibilities. I have a son. Anyway, you
    don't want that fucking luggage, so...

                    RANDY
                , What if I do?

                    CASSIDY
                I can't go there.

                    RANDY
        What about the other day?

                    CASSIDY
                It was a mistake.

                    RANDY
        It didn't feel like a mistake to me.

                    CASSIDY
The club and the real world, they don't mix.

                    RANDY
        I'll tell you, I think that's a lot of
                    bullshit...

                    140

because I think **you** **s**till feel something.

                    CASSIDY
You're a customer, okay? You're a fucking
customer. I don't **go** out with customers.
                You got it!?

A long, wounded pause from **Randy**.

                    RANDY
    Yeah, I got **it**. (to bartender) Can I **have** some
tequila over **here**, please? (back to Cass**i**dy) I **tell**
you **what**, here.

He takes a $20 out of **his** pocket holding it **out** to her.

                    CASSIDY
                What's that?

                    RANDY

        I want a dance.
                    CASSIDY
                Stop it.

                    RANDY
What's the matter? You gonna refuse a customer?

He slides it across the bar to her. She slides it
back.

            RANDY (CONT'D)
    I want a goddamn dance, sweetheart.

                    CASSIDY
            Fuck you!

                    RANDY
Get up there and move your ass, squeeze your tit-
ties together, shake your fucking ass...

                    CASSIDY
            Fuck you!

                    RANDY
    ...and pretend you like me!
        Give me a goddamn dance!

Randy SLAMS his hand down on **the** countertop.

                    CASSIDY

    Get the fuck outta here.

                    BIG CHRIS
            Ram! Let's take it outside.

Randy storms out of the club, humiliated.

                    RANDY (O.S.)
            You want a drink, my man?

                    BIG CHRIS (O.S.)
              No, I'm okay.

Cassidy watches him go. She can barely hold back the
tears.
                    CUT TO:

            INT. VAN - LATER

Randy pulls up to his trailer. He sits there with the
engine idling, staring at his trailer, scared to go
in alone. He pulls back out again.

                    CUT TO:

        INT. RAHWAY REC CENTER - ENTRANCE - LATER

Randy limps in beneath a vinyl banner reading JAPW -
JERSEY ALL-PRO WRESTLING. LARRY COHEN, the promoter,
is at the door collecting tickets.

                    LARRY COHEN
                    Ram!

                    RANDY
              Hey, Larry.

Cohen pulls him in for a hug.

                    LARRY COHEN
        Hey, man, what's happening? What are you doing
            here? I thought you retired.

                    RANDY
        I did. I just came to see the show.

                    LARRY COHEN
        Well, come in. Come on, man.
        Of course. Straight in.

Randy shakes a few hands and walks into:

    INT. RAHWAY REC CENTER - GYMNASIUM - CONTINUOUS

The promotion is **underway**, a **tag** team match finishing up. Randy **climbs** up into the stands and takes a seat.

RON **KILLINGS** (30s), a big wrestler is launching a cheap shot on his opponent, ROMEO ROSELLI. He falls on top of **Romeo** for the pin. **The Ref smacks** the **mat,** counting.

REF&CROWD
One!... Two!...

Up in the stands, Randy watches **them wrestle** off-screen.

Randy's eyes are glued to the action... **Punches. Kicks. Suplexes. Bodyslams.** The crowd **is going** crazy.

He is tempted. Salivating almost.

INT. RAHWAY REC CENTER - **BACKSTAGE** - **LATER**

Randy walks backstage into **the dressing** area. He sees RON KILLINGS and ROMEO **ROSELLI and** walks up to them.

RON
Hey **Ram! What** s up man?

ROMEO
You like it?

RANDY
(in his element)
Yeah, you guys put on a helluva **show.**

RON
Appreciate it man.

ROMEO
(pointing to Ron)
It's 'cause of this guy. This guy.

RON
Nah, it's cause of this guy.

RANDY
Hey. Hey. What's important is that they liked you.

ROMEO
They did, they loved it.

145

                    RON
            So, how you been man?

                    RANDY
        Well, hanging and swinging, brother.

                    RON
    You swinging? Let's go get a couple of drinks?

                    RANDY
            Get a drink? You buying?

                    RON
            I'll buy for you bud.

                CUT TO:

    INT. RAHWAY HOTEL BAR - LATER

A hotel bar, lively and hopping with a weekend
crowd. Ron and Romeo dance with a couple girls
in the background while Randy talks with a young
blonde, ALYSSA.

                    ALYSSA
                    (coy)
            I know who you are.

She downs a shot.

                ALYSSA (CONT'D)
    My brother used to have your poster on his door.

Randy smiles, pleased, takes a shot.

                    RANDY
        Well, your brother's got taste.

                    ALYSSA
    Yeah, it was a pretty hot picture. So what are you
            doing in our town of Rahway?

                    RANDY
        We did a show at the Rec Center tonight.

                    ALYSSA
    Wrestling. Wow, so you still wrestle?

Randy nods and smiles.

                    RANDY
        Still jumping off the top rope. Yeah.

                    146

                    ALYSSA
              Oh, wow, that's hot.

She pauses. Takes him in.

                    ALYSSA (CONT'D)
              So you wanna party?

They exchange a look.

                    RANDY
              Party? What do you call party?

She grabs him and gives him a shake.

                    ALYSSA
              I don't know, party-like-a-fireman party.

                    HARD CUT TO:

INT. WOMEN'S BATHROOM - SHORT TIME LATER

A single-person bathroom. Randy and Alyssa are doing
BUMPS OF COKE.
                    RANDY
              Oh shit that's speedy.

Alyssa pushes up against him and they start making
out.

INT. WOMEN'S BATHROOM - SHORT TIME LATER

Randy is FUCKING Alyssa from behind over the bathroom
sink.

Alyssa MOANS LOUDLY. She sounds like a FIRE ENGINE.

                    ALYSSA
              RRRRRRRRRrrrrr, RRRRRRRrrrrr!

A woman enters and is shocked by the view.

                    WOMAN
              Oh, get a fucking room.

They don't even notice her. Alyssa screams in pleasure.

                    ALYSSA
              Oh, yeah!

                    CUT TO:

INT. BEDROOM - **SHORT TIME LATER**

BLACK **SCREEN.**

RANDY'S POV: His eyes slowly open. Staring down at him from a white stucco ceiling is a poster of a HUNKY, SHIRTLESS **FIREMAN** with a pair of suspenders stretched across his oiled-up six pack. Across the bottom it says FIREMEN LIKE IT HOT!.

Randy looks around, disoriented. He is NAKED in a strange bed in a strange bedroom. There are hunky firemen posters hanging on every wall in the room.

As he sits up out of bed he realizes he is wearing a PAIR OF FIREMEN BOOTS. Alyssa nowhere in sight, Randy quietly dresses.

As he is leaving, a STRANGE SOUND emanates from the corner. Randy lifts up a curtain to reveal a PET FERRET in a cage. It squeaks at him. Weirded out, Randy gets out of there while Alyssa's still in the shower.

EXT. APARTMENT BUILDING - SHORT TIME LATER

Randy emerges from Alyssa's building in the previous night's clothes, squinting at the blinding sunlight.

INT. RANDY'S **TRAILER** - SHORT TIME LATER

Randy enters his trailer, chuckling amusedly. He tosses his keys on the table. And he crashes on his bed.

INT. **RANDY'S TRAILER** - NIGHT

Randy wakes in his clothes from last night.

He heads over to the fridge and grabs a beer. As he closes the fridge, his expression changes. A look of DEEP DISMAY comes over his face.

RANDY'S POV: The old photo of him and Stephanie on the fridge door. Pissed off, Randy snatches his keys and storms out of the trailer.

CUT TO:

EXT. STEPHANIE'S HOUSE - SHORT TIME LATER

148

Randy rings the bell. Stephanie's "friend" answers the door.

She stares at him coldly and unnervingly.

                         RANDY
                Hey, is Stephanie home?

She goes into the house, but fails to shut the door all the way, leaving it open just a crack.

He takes the opportunity to enter, treading softly. From somewhere inside, he hears the MUFFLED SOUND of Stephanie and The Friend talking.

          INT. STEPHANIE'S HOUSE - CONTINUOUS

Randy walks towards the sound of Stephanie and The Friend arguing.

                     THE FRIEND (O.S.)
        Steph? Guess who finally decided to show up? Yeah,
                   he's standing outside.

                     STEPHANIE (O.S.)
                 No, I don't want to do that.

                     THE FRIEND (O.S.)
        I don't want you to be stressed out anymore. Let me
                   get this asshole out of here.

                     STEPHANIE (O.S.)
                 Okay, just don't say anything.

Randy finds them in the kitchen, the friend standing over Stephanie as she sobs, sitting at the table.

                         RANDY
                         Hey.

                       THE FRIEND
                Who said you could come in?

                       STEPHANIE
        What the fuck are you doing in here?

                         RANDY
                I'm so sorry, Stephanie.

                       THE FRIEND
                  Get the fuck out.

> STEPHANIE
> (to The Friend)
> I can handle this. I can handle this.

> THE FRIEND
> Obviously not.

The Friend, disgusted, grabs her coat and STORMS OFF.
Stephanie chases her through the house. Randy follows, mumbling apologies.

> STEPHANIE
> (teeth gritted)
> I can handle this.

> RANDY
> Come on, I'm sorry I screwed this up. I'm so sorry.

> STEPHANIE
> Wait.

You don't have to leave.

The Friend, disgusted, grabs her coat and STORMS OFF
out the front door. Alone, father and daughter.

                    RANDY
               Fuck.

                  STEPHANIE
     You know what? I waited in that restaurant two
     hours. Two fucking hours. Telling myself, "Maybe
     something happened, maybe he got stuck in traf-
     fic..."... But no, you just keep doing the same shit
               to me over and over again!

                    RANDY
     I know, I apologize. I've got a lot of stuff swim-
     ming around in my head. And I went out and had a
        drink and another drink and I just spaced.

                  STEPHANIE
             That is tough shit.

                    RANDY
       Goddamn it. Why do I do this to you?

                  STEPHANIE
     Because you are a fuck-up. You're a walking, liv-
     ing, breathing fuck-up. I cannot fucking do it any-
     more. I can't stand it, I can't fucking cry for you
          anymore, I can't fucking do it anymore...

She grabs a SMALL POTTED PLANT off the table and
FLINGS IT AT HIM. It smashes into him.

> STEPHANIE (CONT'D)
> You are a fucking asshole.

She grabs a CAN OF SODA off the same table.

> STEPHANIE (CONT'D)
> (throwing can)
> You're an asshole! You're a fucking asshole!
> Go fuck yourself!

The can NAILS HIM IN THE HEAD, exploding open on the
floor. Soda sprays everywhere.

He rushes toward her, wrapping her up in his arms.

> RANDY
> Calm down. Calm down.

She THRASHES AROUND, fighting it. He SQUEEZES TIGHTER,
pulling her gently to the floor.

> STEPHANIE
> Do not touch me! I fucking hate you!

> RANDY
> I'm sorry. I know you hate me. I know you do.

Suddenly, she STOPS RESISTING. A STRANGE AND UNEX-
PECTED CALM washes over her.

> STEPHANIE
> You know what? I don't care.

She is silent and still.

She shakes her head, placidly gazing off.

> STEPHANIE (CONT'D)
> I don't hate you. I don't love you. I don't even
> like you. And I was stupid to think you could
> change.

> RANDY
> I can change.

> STEPHANIE
> I don't care.

                              RANDY
                            Come on.

                            STEPHANIE
          There is no more fixing it. It's broke. Permanently.
              And I'm ok with that. It's better.

                              RANDY
                   I'm sorry. I'm really sorry.

                            STEPHANIE
                 I don't ever want to see you again.

          She turns and looks him in the eye.

                        STEPHANIE (CONT'D)
          Look at me. I don't wanna see you, I don't want to
              hear you. I'm done. Do you understand?

          Crying, Randy nods. She walks toward the front door.
          Opens it wide.

                        STEPHANIE (CONT'D)
                          Get out.

          Randy slowly gets up and steps out the front door.

                  EXT. STEPHANIE'S HOUSE - CONTINUOUS

          Randy steps out the front door. Stephanie closes the
          door behind him. Randy stands there alone. Unsure
          what to do. He walks slowly towards his van.

                            CUT TO:

                  INT. ACME - DELI COUNTER - DAY

          About 10 CUSTOMERS hover in front of the DELI COUNTER
          clutching Take-A-Number tickets.

          Randy, manning the counter with a COWORKER, hands a
          WOMAN a packet of roast beef.

                              RANDY
                              27!

          An OLD LADY steps forward.

                            OLD LADY
              Pound of German potato salad, please.

Randy grabs a container and starts scooping potato
salad. He puts the container on the scale. It reads
1.06 LB.

> OLD LADY (CONT'D)
> A little less.

Randy scoops out a little.

> RANDY
> A little less.

He weighs it again. The scale reads .96 LB.

> OLD LADY
> A little more.

Randy puts a little more in.

> RANDY
> A little more.

The scale reads 1.03.

> OLD LADY
> A little less.

> RANDY
> A little less?

Randy, trying to contain his aggravation, turns his
back and eats a couple wedges of potato.

He returns to the scale. It now reads 1.00.

> RANDY (CONT'D)
> A little less.

> OLD LADY
> (rolls her eyes)
> At last.

Wayne notices the aggravated customers.

> WAYNE
> What's with the line?

Wayne gives a QUICK CLAP at Randy.

> WAYNE (CONT'D)
> Let's pick it up alright. It's rush hour.

Randy slaps a price sticker on the container and hands it across the counter.

                    RANDY
                  (sarcastic)
              Have a nice day.

She shuffles off with her potato salad.

                    RANDY (CONT'D)
                Number 31!

A BLUE-COLLAR GUY (40s) steps forward.

                    CUSTOMER
          31. Yeah, could I get a...

The guy does a DOUBLE-TAKE, noticing Randy's face.

                    CUSTOMER (CONT'D)
          Do I know you from somewheres?

                    RANDY
                  No.

The guy studies Randy's face, trying hard to place it.

                    CUSTOMER
            You look so damn familiar.
                (racking his brain)
                You Teamsters?

                    RANDY
            What are you having?

                    CUSTOMER
        Can I get a half pound of Virginia ham and a half
            pound of the Jarlsberg?

Randy reaches into the case and pulls out a ham.

                    CUSTOMER (O.S.) (CONT'D)
            I know we've met someplace.

He brings it over to the slicer, his back turned away from the guy.

                    CUSTOMER (O.S.) (CONT'D)
                You play softball?

                         RANDY
                          No.

                    CUSTOMER (O.S.)
       You're not one of Mikey Bosch's buddies, right?

                         RANDY
                 Never heard of the guy.

He turns on the electric slicer and begins.

Slice, slice...

The guy SNAPS HIS FINGERS.

                       CUSTOMER
                    Wait a second.

He looks at Randy, surprised and amazed.

                    CUSTOMER (CONT'D)
                    Randy The Ram?

Slice, slice...

                    CUSTOMER (CONT'D)
              The wrestler from the '80s?
                    (forms Ram horns)
                   Ram Jam!
                         RANDY
                    No.
                    CUSTOMER (O.S.)
                 Wow, that's freaky.

ANGLE ON the block of cheese as Randy slices. There's
only a SMALL CHUNK left. The chunk dwindles, getting
smaller and smaller. He watches as his thumb inches
closer to the spinning blade.

                    CUSTOMER (CONT'D)
         You look just like the dude. 'cept older.

Randy stops slicing. He stares at his thumb. At the
blade. His thumb.

He JAMS HIS THUMB INTO THE BLADE.

Blood squirts everywhere. On his coat.

On the deli meat.

                              RANDY
                         Goddamn it.

Randy stares at the DEEP GASH, watching as blood
pulses out in crimson surges.

A customer GASPS. A commotion quickly spreads.

                         WAYNE (O.S.)
                    Randy, the customer!

Randy turns and sees a shocked Wayne rushing toward
him. Wayne takes Randy's arm and tries to lead him
into the back, out of view.

                      WAYNE (CONT'D)
            (conscious of customers watching)
                  Let's get that patched up.

Randy roughly SHOVES him away. Wayne stumbles back-
wards.

                             RANDY
              You little prick, you're gonna talk to me
                 the way you do? I quit. Alright?

Randy, turning toward the onlookers, raises his thumb
to his face. He dramatically smears the BLOOD ACROSS
HIS MOUTH.

                        RANDY (CONT'D)
                 Want some fucking cheese lady?
                 Get your own fucking cheese.

Customers GASP. A woman SHRIEKS.

Randy dashes down an aisle. He dodges a WOMAN PUSHING
A SHOPPING CART, purposely "over-dodging" her so he
CRASHES INTO THE SHELVES and sends stuff flying. He
dodges ANOTHER SHOPPER, dramatically crashing into
the shelves again.

                        RANDY (CONT'D)
                    Goddamn it, I quit!

He strips off his apron, rips off his hair net, and
slams an elbow into some cereal boxes. He shoulder
slams another display. He dodges ANOTHER SHOPPER,
crashing into the shelves again.

                  INT. VAN - SHORT TIME LATER

                              159

Randy sits in the van in the Acme parking lot. He wraps his thumb in cloth to stop the bleeding. He gazes at himself in the **rear**-view **mirror**, dried blood caked on his face.

                         RANDY
              (chuckling, to his reflection)
         Oh... Robin. Robin. Man, its Randy. Randy.

                        CUT TO:

EXT. MIELEVILLE - PAY PHONE - LATER

Randy is on the pay phone. His day planner open in his hand,

                         RANDY
               Listen. I **wanna** do it.
                        (beat)
               I want **back in**. **Fanfest**.
                        (beat)
               Just tell him it's back on.
                        (beat)
               Hey, man, I don't give a shit.
               I just wanna wrestle. That's right.
                        (beat)
               Okay. You got it, brother.

INT. **RANDY'**S TRAILER - BATHROOM - LATER

MUSIC: ACCEPT - "BALLS TO THE WALL"

Randy, wearing rubber **gloves** and a towel around his **neck**, combs PEROXIDE through his hair.

INT. RANDY'S TRAILER - **BATHROOM** - LATER

Randy is SHAVING HIS ARMPITS. The hair has grown in since he last wrestled.

INT. RANDY'S **TRAILER** - BATHROOM - LATER

In his hands is a product called TAN IN A **CAN**. He gives the can a good shake and starts **spraying** his body.

INT. RANDY'S TRAILER - BATHROOM - LATER

Randy **washes** and dries his hair. He lifts **some** weights, towel still wrapped around his head. Randy **puts** on his RAM HORN NECKLACE.

CUT TO:

INT. CASSIDY'S APARTMENT - CONTINUOUS

Cassidy finishes cleaning up in the bathroom and heads
out into the living room. Cassidy grabs her purse and
car keys off the kitchen table.

CASSIDY
In bed by 11. I don't want him to bargain.

The BABYSITTER (15) nods at the instructions. Cassidy
heads toward the Living room.

CASSIDY (CONT'D)
Bye, monkey...

She is struck by what she sees.

CASSIDY'S POV: JAMESON (9) is on the floor, playing
with the Randy The Ram doll.

She watches as he makes the Randy doll climb up the
couch's armrest. The doll takes a FLYING LEAP off the
couch, onto a STAR WARS FIGURE laid out on the floor
below. Daniel makes an EXPLOSION SOUND as Randy slams
down on his foe.

Cassidy looks at the doll, worried.

JAMESON
One! Two! Three! You're out, yeahhhh!

EXT. RANDY'S TRAILER - SHORT TIME LATER

Randy puts a snacks-and-soda-filled plastic bag in the
front of the van. He is surprised to see Cassidy pull
up in her car. She gets out.

CASSIDY
Hi.

RANDY
How'd you find me?

CASSIDY
Big Chris.

RANDY
Big Chris?

                         CASSIDY
                    Cheeques bouncer.

Randy nods oh.

                         CASSIDY (CONT'D)
                    Look, I know I came off like a bitch the
                    other day and I'm really sorry. I didn't
                    mean all those things that I said. You're
                         not just a customer...

Randy nods, waits for her to finish.

                         CASSIDY (CONT'D)
                    But, you know, at the same time, I have
                         this line, and I just...
                         I can't cross it.

                         RANDY
                    No, I understand that. That's okay.

He climbs into the driver's seat and shuts the
door.

                         RANDY (CONT'D)
                         I gotta go.

                         CASSIDY
                    Where are you going?

                         RANDY
                    I got a match.

                         CASSIDY
                         A match?

He hands her a FANFEST FLIER.

                         RANDY
                    It's in Wilmington. Come by.

He DRIVES OFF, not giving her time to reply.

                         CASSIDY
                    (as he's pulling out)
                    When is it? What...

He DRIVES OFF. She watches him go, the van kicking up
dust in its wake.

She looks at flier. A look of concern comes over her
face.

INT. VAN - EVENING

MUSIC: ACCEPT - "BALLS TO THE WALL"

Randy is driving south on the New Jersey Turnpike.

INT. WILMINGTON RIALTO THEATER - ENTRYWAY - LATER

Randy enters the ARENA with his wheelie bag.

BOB "THE AYATOLLAH" ZAYID (52) stands ringside talking to wrestler NIGEL MCGUINNESS (32).

> THE AYATOLLAH
> Phoenix is not out of the question. I'm
> taking over Arizona, you hear me?

> NIGEL MCGUINNESS
> (not too interested)
> Looks like it.

The Ayatollah looks up and sees Randy looking at him.

> THE AYATOLLAH
> Ram-A-Lam.

Randy heads over.

> RANDY
> Hey Bob.

> NIGEL MCGUINNESS
> What's up man?

> RANDY
> (hugs Nigel)
> Hey Nigel. How you doing brother? Long time.
> (hugs Bob)
> Hey look out.

> THE AYATOLLAH
> Good to see ya, bro. You know what, I didn't think
> we were gonna do this.

> RANDY
> Yeah? You and everybody else.

> THE AYATOLLAH
> Sunday night, I get a call and they say "He's back
> in! It's on again." I'm like "What?"

WRESTLING

NICK VOLPI PRESENTS FANFEST in association with

ROH
RING OF HONOR

FRI APRIL 6

RANDY ROBINSON

MAIN EVENT

THE RAM

THE **-VS-** REMATCH

AYATOLLAH

20 YEAR ANNIVERSARY

7:00 PM SHARP

Nigel McGuiness

ALSO SCHEDULED TO APPEAR

TAKESHI

NO REMORSE CORP

LOC

"THE DREAM"

COLT CABANA

DEVITO

HOMOCIDE

+ MANY MORE

WILMINGTON RIALTO THEATRE-WILMINGTON DELAWARE

The Ayatollah chortles.

                    RANDY
    So listen, when you get settled in, we should go
              over some of the things.

                 THE AYATOLLAH
                  What things?

                    RANDY
               Some of the spots.

                 THE AYATOLLAH
    Okay, how's about this right here: I'm the heel,
              you're the face. Done.

                    RANDY
    Hey, Bob. I'm glad to see things haven't changed.

The Ayatollah chuckles.

                 THE AYATOLLAH
             Yeah, I love you too.

Randy walks off, highly annoyed.

                 THE AYATOLLAH (CONT'D)
                   (to Nigel)
    Now, back to you. What kind of car do you want man?

                 NIGEL MCGUINNESS
        I don't know, something affordable.

                 THE AYATOLLAH
            How about something pink?

             INT. CHEEQUES- LATER

    MUSIC: SCORPIONS - "ANIMAL MAGNETISM"

Cassidy is dancing on stage. She has a distracted,
faraway look in her eye.

She abruptly WALKS OFF mid-song.

She heads toward the dressing room, disappearing
through the curtain.

                 CLUB D.J. (O.S.)
    Cassidy. Come on Cassidy, get back up there.
              They're not done with you yet.

INT. DRESSING AREA - CONTINUOUS

Cassidy unzips her roller bag and jams in her stuff.
She gets dressed, pulls on her boots, grabs her bag
and jacket and walks towards the main room. Another
DANCER calls out after her.

                    DANCER
          You left your shoes.

Cassidy ignores her, keeps going. The DJ calls out
over the loudspeaker.

                    CLUB D.J.
          Cassidy. Cassidy! Hey Pam!

She cuts across the room, toward the exit.

          EXT. CHEEQUES- CONTINUOUS

Cassidy steps out of the club.

                    CASSIDY
                   (to self)
                    Pam.

          INT. WILMINGTON RIALTO THEATER
             - LOCKER ROOM - LATER

Randy looks at a large FANFEST POSTER on the wall.
The ROH card is underway. Through a wall, we hear the
muffled sounds of a MATCH IN PROGRESS: cheers, boos,
crashes, etc.

Randy, sitting alone on a bench in just his jock
strap,· tapes up his legs. His focus and intensity
build

          INT. GAS STATION - SHORT TIME LATER

Cassidy pulls into a gas station. She rolls down the
window.

                    GAS STATION ATTENDANT
          Three more miles.

He points in the right direction.

                    GAS STATION ATTENDANT
                   (CONT'D)
          Three more miles.

Cassidy waves and speeds off.

INT. LOCKER ROOM - LATER

Randy, suited up in his tights, paces the floor, gearing himself up for the match. The only other wrestler in the locker room at the moment is The Ayatollah, doing neck rolls nearby. ARABIC MUSIC plays in the background, the RING ANNOUNCER starts to call out the match.

ANNOUNCER
Weighing in at 252 pounds, the Tehran Terror...

RANDY
Ready to do this?

THE AYATOLLAH
I think so, I'll see you out there.

The Ayatollah grabs a large IRANIAN FLAG leaning against the lockers. He heads toward an ENTRANCE CURTAIN.

ANNOUNCER (O.S.)
(through curtain)
...the Beast Of The Middle East...
(beat)
The Ayaaa-tooo-laaaaaah!

INT. WILMINGTON RIALTO THEATER - ENTRYWAY
- SHORT TIME LATER

Cassidy rushes down the hallway towards the TICKETING TABLE.

CASSIDY
Hey, hey, hey. How much? How much?

TICKET SELLER
20 Dollars.

She forks it over.

INT. AUDITORIUM - CONTINUOUS

The Ayatollah saunters down the ramp towards the ring waving his Iranian flag to boos and jeers from the crowd.

INT. AUDITORIUM - OUTER CONCOURSE - CONTINUOUS

Cassidy enters the concourse crowded with fans. Frantic, she asks a vendor at a souvenir table for help.

                    CASSIDY
              Which way's backstage?

The vendor points to the back, Cassidy makes her way around the edge of the crowd to a SECURITY GUARD standing by a curtain.

                  CASSIDY (CONT'D)
       Can I get back there? This is backstage?

                SECURITY GUARD
                  Right there.

Cassidy heads through the curtain.

     INT. BACKSTAGE DRESSING ROOM - CONTINUOUS

Randy looks in the mirror, touching his chest scar gingerly. Eyes closed he prays, crosses himself, and then smacks his padded-elbow into his fist.

        INT. BACKSTAGE HALLWAY

Cassidy runs through a hallway filled with prop lights, wires, etc.

        INT. LOCKER ROOM - CONTINUOUS

Randy is peering through the narrow gap in the curtain, watching The Ayatollah make his entrance.

                 CASSIDY (O.S.)
                    Randy.

Randy, turning, is surprised to see Cassidy standing there. She looks tired and worried and scared.

                 CASSIDY (CONT'D)
                     Hey.

                    RANDY
        Hey, what are you doing here?

                   CASSIDY
        What the fuck are you doing?

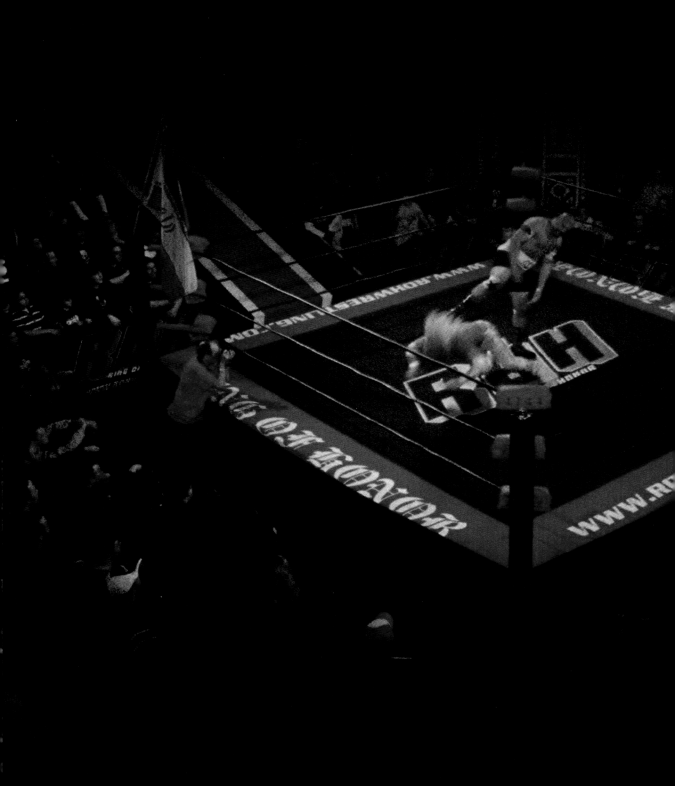

                              RANDY
              I'm doing my thing. I'm going to work.

                             CASSIDY
                       Yeah, but your heart?

                              RANDY
                  My heart? My heart's still ticking.

                             CASSIDY
                     Yeah but the doctor said...

                              RANDY
                            (chuckling)
              I know what I'm doing. And, you know, the only
                  place I get hurt is out there.

Randy becomes serious.

                         RANDY (CONT'D)
                  The world don't give a shit about me.

                             CASSIDY
                  I'm here. What do you call that?

Randy looks at her, briefly vulnerable.

                       CASSIDY (CONT'D)
                  I'm really here. What do you call that?

Through the curtain, we hear the Arabic music DIE DOWN.

A new, familiar song rises on the auditorium speakers.

     MUSIC: GUNS 'N' ROSES - "SWEET CHILD O' MINE"

The crowd roars.

                         ANNOUNCER (O.S.)
              And his opponent, from Elizabeth, New Jersey weigh-
              ing in at 225 pounds, a true wrestling immortal...

                              RANDY
                        (points to curtain)
              You hear them? This is where is where I belong.

                         ANNOUNCER (O.S.)
                  ...Randy "The Ram" Robinson!

                              RANDY
                          I gotta go.

He turns away, heads toward the curtain.

                         CASSIDY
                  No, no. Randy. Randy!

              INT. AUDITORIUM - CONTINUOUS

Randy bursts through the curtain to HUGE CHEERS. The
place is packed with 1,000 plus people. Randy, a smile
on his face, saunters down the ramp, slapping fans'
hands. He takes a long lap around the ring, giving out
high five after high five. The fans eat it up.

Randy climbs into the ring, where The Ayatollah
awaits.

The cheers continue. Loving, appreciative, sustained
cheers. Randy stands there soaking it in, basking in
their love.

He grabs the microphone from the ring announcer. He
looks around. A hush comes over the crowd.

              BACKSTAGE CURTAIN:

Cassidy looks on from the narrow slit in the curtain.

                   IN THE RING:

Randy looks out at the crowd, collecting his
thoughts.

                          RANDY
        I just want to say to you all tonight I'm very
     grateful to be here. A lot of people told me that
     I'd never wrestle again... well, that's all I do.
      You know if you live hard, and you play hard and
     you burn the candle at both ends, you pay the price
     for it. You know, in this life, you can lose everything
         that you love and everything that loves you.

Looking on, Cassidy tears up.

                     RANDY (CONT'D)
     Now, I don't hear as good as I used to, and I for-
     get stuff, and I ain't as pretty as I used to be,
      but goddamn it, I'm still standing here, and I'm
     the Ram. As time goes by they say, "He's washed up,
     he's finished. He's a loser. He's all through." But
     you know what? The only ones who are gonna tell me
     when I'm through doing my thing is you people here.

Randy points to the crowd.

                    RANDY (CONT'D)
You people here... You people here are the ones who
are worth bringing it for because you're my family.
      I love all of you. Thank you so much.

Randy lowers the mic, finished. The fans CHEER WILDLY,
the loudest cheers yet.

              BACK STAGE CURTAIN:

Cassidy, still crying, watches, concerned.

                 IN THE RING:

Randy and the Ayatollah shake hands.

                  THE AYATOLLAH
                  Great job, man.

Randy goes to his corner, nodding appreciatively at
the crowd, The Ayatollah SNEAKS UP BEHIND HIM and
gives him a HARD CHOP to the back.

Randy goes down. The match is on.

The Ayatollah has Randy pinned in a corner against
the ropes, slapping him relentlessly.

              BACKSTAGE CURTAIN:

Cassidy winces. She can't take this any longer.
Crying, she turns from the curtain and walks away.

                 IN THE RING:

The Ayatollah chokes Randy. Randy breaks free, jumps
up and throws his legs over the Ayatollah's shoulders. Using his weight he drops down, flinging his
opponent to the mat.

Thrown for a loop, the Ayatollah staggers back into
the opposite corner. Randy attacks, his punches and
elbows connecting with the stunned Ayatollah. Not for
long, as the Ayatollah curls his arms around Randy's
head, putting it in a vice grip.

                  THE AYATOLLAH (CONT'D)
                  (under breath)
                  Take it easy.

The Ayatollah, boxes Randy's ears, Randy staggers back, clutching his head in mock-pain, his long hair flailing about for added effect. The Ayatollah, arms raised, charges at The Ram, but Randy is waiting for him and gives him a shot to the gut. Randy throws The Ayatollah into the ropes, waiting with outstretched arm to clothesline him. The Ayatollah goes down, rolling onto his stomach, stunned.

Randy crouches over his opponent, pulling his arms back and his chin up. The notorious "camel-clutch."

                    THE AYATOLLAH (CONT'D)
          What are you doing? This is my move!

The Referee crouches down.

                         REFEREE
                    (to The Ayatollah)
               You wanna give up?

Reversing the move, The Ayatollah backs out from under Randy's legs and throws him over his shoulders, onto the mat, then takes position above Randy to perform "His" move. He grabs Randy's chin, pulling up, choking Randy.

                    THE AYATOLLAH
       You steal my move Randy, this is how you do it!

Randy grabs for the ropes, saving himself on a technicality. The Ref calls it.

                         REFEREE
               One! Two! Three!

Angered, The Ayatollah gets up and shoves the Ref into the ropes.

                    REFEREE (CONT'D)
          Who you pushing? Come on, I'm the referee, you
                    can't push me!

                    THE AYATOLLAH
          Don't tell me what to do!

The Ayatollah winds up to hit the Ref, but as he swings Randy pushes the Ref aside, taking the blow squarely on the jaw. He goes down. The Ayatollah pushes off the ropes for momentum, runs at Randy, and flattens him with a HARD KICK to the back.

THE CROWD BOOS. Randy writhes around feigning semi-consciousness. The Ayatollah raises his hands, challenging the crowd. He grabs his Iranian flag from the corner of the ring, waving it tauntingly. They respond with boos and chants of USA! USA!

Randy tries to get up but The Ayatollah hits him over the head with the flag pole. He takes the butt end of the pole and JABS IT into Randy's back. Randy grimaces in pain.

The Ayatollah takes his flag, sticks it under Randy's chin and JERKS UP, lifting him up off the mat by his neck, strangling him. Randy THRASHES AROUND, fighting for breath, grasping at the pole.

> THE AYATOLLAH (CONT'D)
> (leaning in)
>
> I forgot how much fun this was, Ram!

> RANDY
> (though his teeth)
>
> Bring it, Bob!

Randy resists, fighting against The Ayatollah in a tideturning battle of sheer strength. He slowly pushes the pole away from his neck, up over his head and throws a surprised Ayatollah over his shoulder.

Randy stands up, triumphant, and breaks the flag over his knee, throwing the pieces into the crowd.

> RANDY (CONT'D)
> (to The Ayatollah)
>
> Asshole!

> THE AYATOLLAH
>
> Infidel!

The Ayatollah charges at Randy, who ducks out of the way, sending him over the ropes to the concrete floor below. Randy pushes off and leaps over the top rope, crashing down on The Ayatollah and the Referee. The crowd goes wild, chanting HOLY SHIT! HOLY SHIT!

> OUTSIDE THE RING:-

Randy stands, helps the Ref up.

> RANDY
>
> Hey, you ok Ref?

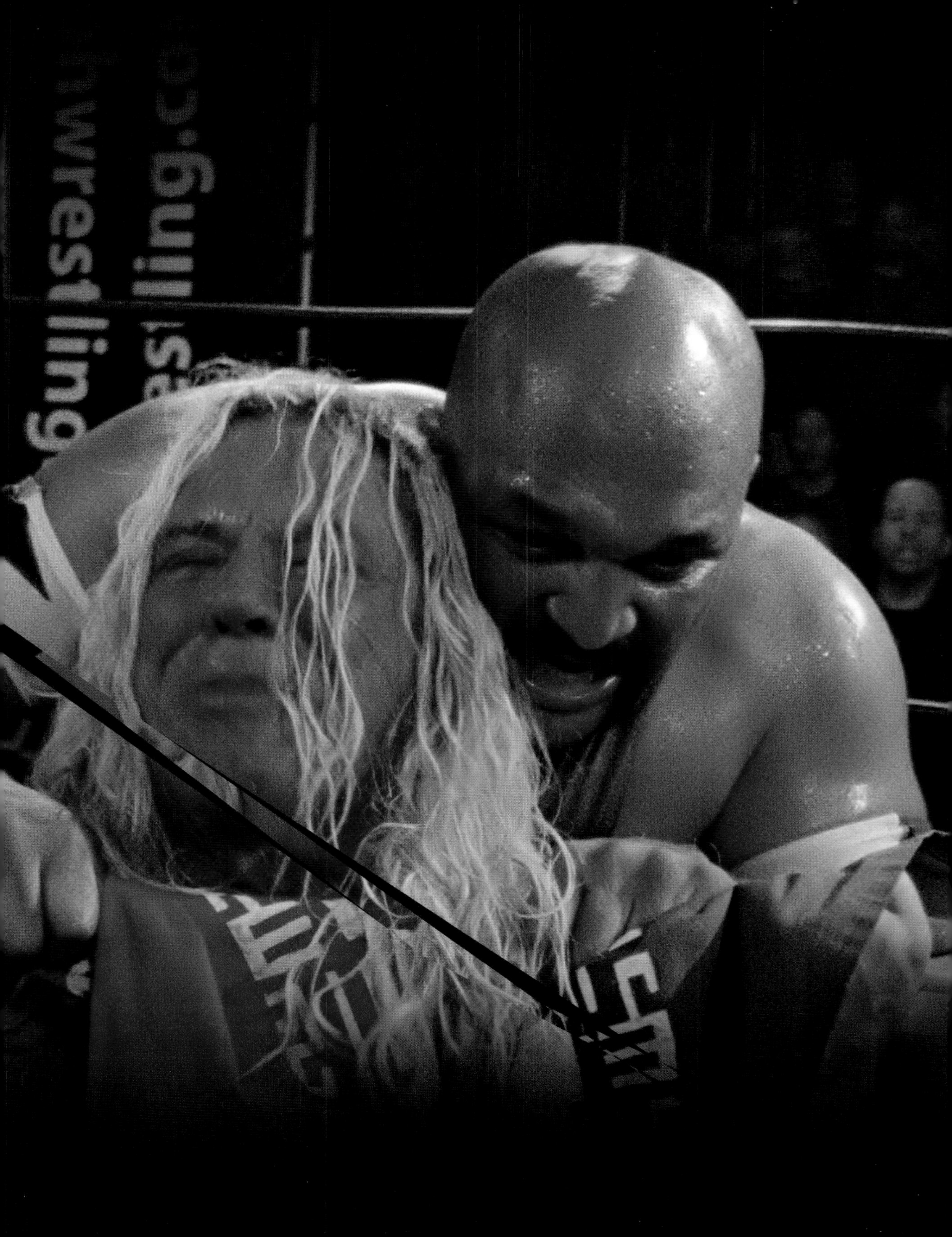
wrestling

His back turned, The Ayatollah gets up and gives him
a HARD CHOP across the back, and then grabs him and
throws him headfirst into the METAL CORNER POST.

Picking up Randy by the hair, The Ayatollah threatens
to use him as a battering ram on the crowd.

> THE AYATOLLAH
> (pointing at a fan)
> Now I'm gonna take you out baby!

But Randy reverses, throwing The Ayatollah headfirst
into the metal barrier separating the fans from the
ringside area. CLANG! The Ayatollah goes down.

Randy's clutches his chest. HIS HEART IS POUNDING.
He takes a breath and fights through it, the crowd
cheering wildly in the background. Randy picks up the
Ayatollah...

> THE AYATOLLAH (CONT'D)
> (under breath)
> Let's take it home.

...And throws him into the ring, jumping up onto
the ropes after him. As The Ayatollah approaches
Randy SWINGS HIS LEGS up over the top rope and onto
The Ayatollah's shoulders, putting him in a SCISSOR
HEAD LOCK. Randy pushes off, dropping his weight and
throwing the Ayatollah into the mat.

He clotheslines the stunned Ayatollah but on the
follow through his HEART LURCHES and Randy doubles
over, again clutching his chest.

> THE AYATOLLAH (CONT'D)
> Ram? Are you all right?

Randy nods, grabs The Ayatollah's head and slams it
into the corner post, then swings him around and
throws him into the far post. Randy charges, but mid-
charge his HEART LURCHES AGAIN and he falls to one
knee, grimacing in pain. He struggles to breathe.

> THE AYATOLLAH (CONT'D)
> Ram?

Through the pain Randy motions to him to continue.

> THE AYATOLLAH (CONT'D)
> (under his breath)

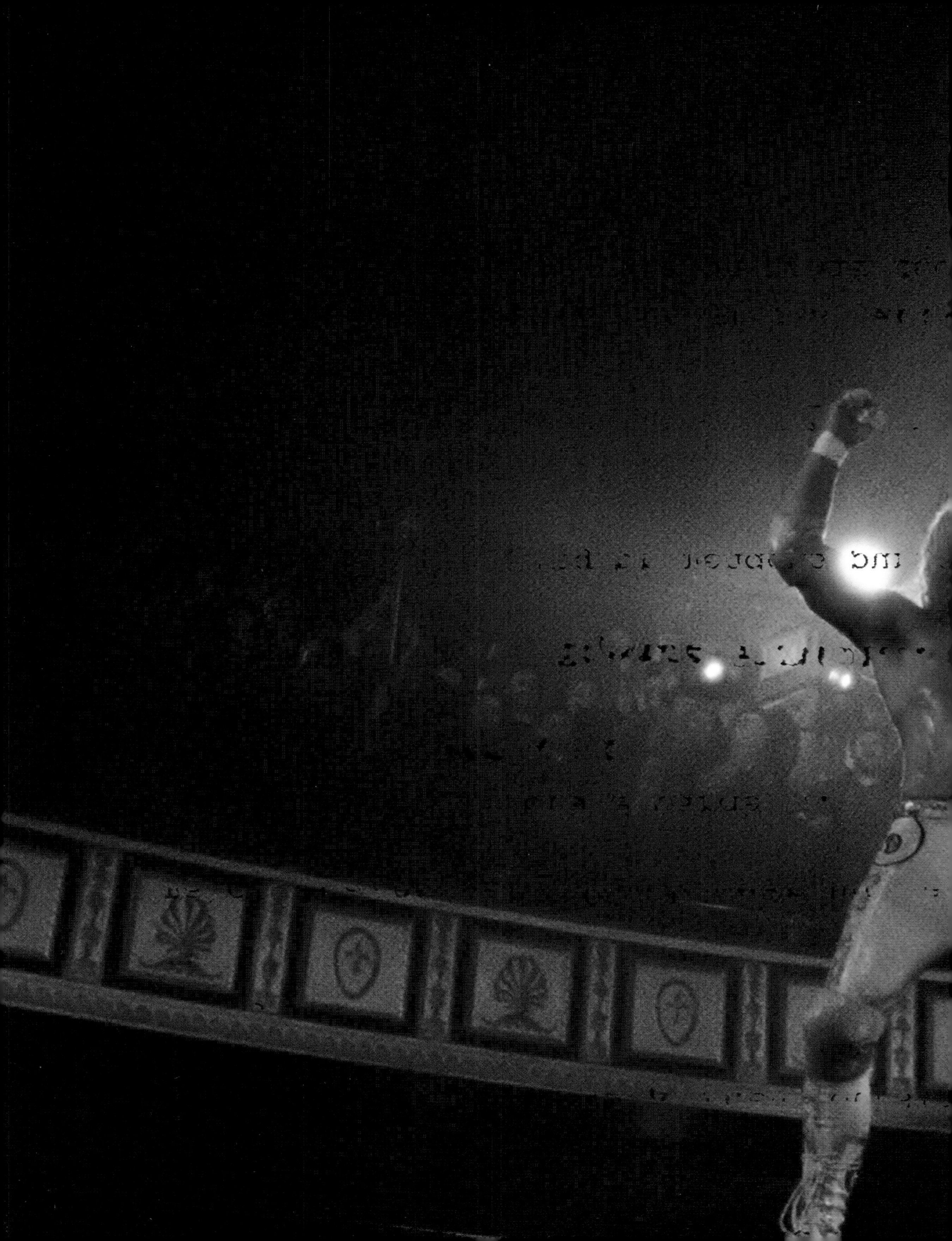

I'll take it from here.

The Ayatollah runs and flips over Randy's shoulder, selling it like he was tripped and thrown.

> THE AYATOLLAH (CONT'D)
> (lying on the mat)
> Pin me! C'mon Ram, pin me!

Randy struggles, pushing himself up. He can barely breathe. He stumbles around the ring, looking around at the hungry crowd, and down at his chest, bewildered.

> THE AYATOLLAH (CONT'D)
> It's okay, Ram. Take it home.

Randy regains composure enough to SUPER KICK The Ayatollah, knocking him to the mat.

The fans sense it's near the end. The entire crowd is on its feet. A chant rises:

> CROWD (O.S.)
> Ram Jam! Ram Jam! Ram Jam!...

Randy climbs through the ropes, preparing for his signature move. Torn, his eyes drift in Cassidy's direction.

HIS POV: Cassidy is gone.

Randy bows his head in disappointment. He turns to the corner post and starts to climb. The crowd's chants and cheers grow louder and louder. They are hungry for the Ram Jam.

Randy raises his arms, presses his fists against his head to form a set of ram's horns.

The crowd CHEERS.

Randy leaps.

END.

First published in the United States of America in 2009 by
Rizzoli International Publications, Inc.
300 Park Avenue South
New York, NY 10010

www.rizzoliusa.com

2009 2010 2011 2012 2013 / 10 9 8 7 6 5 4 3 2 1

Rizzoli Editor: Jessica Fuller

Book Created by Hi-ReS!
Art Direction: Florian Schmitt
Design: Anthony Sheret
Producer: Andrew Duffus
www.hi-res.net

Printed in the U.S.
ISBN-13: 978-0-8478-3243-9
Library of Congress Catalog Control Number: 2008941690

FOX SEARCHLIGHT PICTURES PRESENTS
in association with WILD BUNCH
a PROTOZOA PICTURES PRODUCTION
a film by DARREN ARONOFSKY

MICKEY ROURKE
MARISA TOMEI
and EVAN RACHEL WOOD

Casting by	Production Designer
MARY VERNIEU, CSA	TIMOTHY GRIMES
SUZANNE SMITH-CROWLEY	Director of Photography
Music Supervisor	MARYSE ALBERTI
JIM BLACK	Executive Producers
Original Score	VINCENT MARAVAL
CLINT MANSELL	AGNES MENTRE
Costume Designer	JENNIFER ROTH
AMY WESTCOTT	Produced by
Co-Producer	SCOTT FRANKLIN
MARK HEYMAN	
Editor	Written by
ANDREW WEISBLUM	ROBERT SIEGEL

Directed and Produced by
DARREN ARONOFSKY